# Dr. Phuong Le Callaway's Kitchen

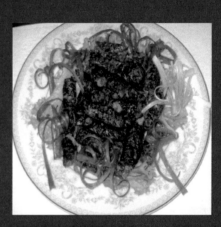

# Dedication

This cookbook is dedicated to the two Generals of the U.S. Air Force and their wives, Lieutenant General (USAF-RET) and Mrs. John E. Jackson, Jr. and Brigadier General (USAF) and Mrs. Ed "Hertz" Vaughan. This cookbook is a personal tribute to them for their long-term support, friendship and mentorship.

Proceeds from the sales, if any, will benefit Fork Union Military Academy and Air Force Aid Society.

# Dr. Phuong Le Callaway's Kitchen

Each recipe and photos are originated from her kitchen and reflect her day-to-day and special occasions cooking for practicality, appeal, and taste for family and friends.

# Acknowledgements

A deep appreciation to my family, friends and to supporters who always make themselves available to provide guidance and support, friendship love and believe in me.

My late mother has been an inspirational figure throughout my life. She was a wonderful woman who has very high expectations for her children, especially her expectations for her daughter to have a happy kitchen.

Happy Kitchen!

*Phuong Le Callaway, Ph.D., CA*
*Friend of Fork Union Military Academy*
*and Air Force Aid Society*

# Vegetables & Herbs

| | | | |
|---|---|---|---|
| Mint | Cilantro/ Coriander | Vietnamese Perilla (tia-to) | Green Papaya http://importfood.com/media/green_papaya_l.jpg |
| Asian Sweet Basil | Japanese Perilla, Red Leaf | Fish Mint | Baby Corn |
| Chinese Leek | Oriental (Daikon) Radish | Watermelon (Hybrid Asia Sweet) | Star Anise |
| Hot Pepper | Oriental Sweet Basil | Garlic | Ginger Roots |

# Description of Some Ingredients

- **Mint**--A very unique herb, called Kinh-Gioi in Vietnam and also often referred to as Vietnamese Balm or Vietnamese Mint in the West. Mint plants produce bright green, saw-edged leaves with lemony scent flavor. The young leaves are used in fish and chicken dishes, salads, soups, and tea. It has been reported that the Vietnamese also drink tea made by boiling water with fresh or dried leaves for medicinal uses. Mint plants grow very well in a sunny and warm area. Young leaves and tips can be harvested 30 days after transplanting. The plants grow to about 20 inches on average. This variety produces many branches and is very productive. It is a good variety for open field planting and container growing. (http://www.evergreenseeds.com/vimikigivba.html).

- **Cilantro/Coriander**--This herb is a tall standing plant, which is slow in bolting. The plants grow well in mild and subtropical climates. Its young leaves and stems have a relatively mild aroma and are good for salads and garnishes. (http://www.evergreenseeds.com/corchinpar.html)

- **Japanese Perilla, Red Leaf**-- Red Perilla is very popular for pickling in Japan. The red leaves are slightly crinkled and makes an attractive bedding plant during summer. (http://www.evergreenseeds.com/redleafak.html)

- **Vietnamese Perilla (tia-to)**-- Tia To (or called Tiet To) is a Vietnamese version of Hojiso, with slightly smaller leaves but a much stronger aromatic flavor. Leaves have green color on the top side and purplish red on the bottom side. The strong flavors are perfect for shrimp or fish dishes. The aromatic leaves are also widely used in pickling. Plants grow best in a sunny location, and the young leaves can be harvested in 30 days after transplanting. Easy to grown, the plants can be grown in open fields or in a container as a wonderful ornamental plant in the backyard. (http://www.evergreenseeds.com/vipeitto.html).

# Description of Some Ingredients

- **Fish Mint (Chameleon Plant)**--This Vietnamese edible variety is all green (non-variegated), unlike most ornamental Chameleon varieties of the same botanical family. The leaves are slightly heart shaped, with small, white flowers. Fish Mint is not commonly used in American-Vietnamese restaurant dishes because of the bold fishy flavors, but it is very popular in home dishes of grilled meats or fish soup dishes. It can be eaten raw in herb noodle salads and fresh home-made fresh spring rolls. For medicinal uses, the leaves are used to treat stomach aches, indigestion, and swellings. The leaves are crushed to a paste to cure insect bites, rashes, and itching. Its native to Japan, Southern China, and Southeast Asia. (http://vietherbs.com/herb-directory/fish-herb).

- **Papaya**-Papayas are spherical or pear-shaped fruits that can be as long as 20 inches. The ones commonly found in the market usually average about 7 inches and weigh about one pound. The fruit, as well as the other parts of the papaya tree, contain papain, an enzyme that helps digest proteins. This enzyme is especially concentrated in the fruit when it is unripe. Papain is extracted to make digestive enzyme dietary supplements. It iss also used as an ingredient in some chewing gums. (http://www.whfoods.com/genpage).

- **Baby Corn**-- Chinese baby corn is a relatively new vegetable. Tender and sweet, baby corn is often used in Chinese dishes and salads. The seeds are sown in spring and are cultivated like regular sweet corn. Many regular corn varieties have been used to grow baby corns, but they often are of a poor quality. The corn ears should be picked for use within 5 days once it starts silking. If not harvested at this stage, the corn ears will develop into full size regular corn. (http://www.evergreenseeds.com/babycorn.html).

- **Chinese Leek**--This vegetable was developed and is grown mainly for harvesting the young flower stems and buds for vegetable dishes. It has relatively small leaves, but it can produce flowers all year round in subtropical and tropical areas. Young flower stems/buds are picked to use as vegetables before flowers begin to blossom. For getting the best eating quality, do not delay the harvesting time. The plants' performance may be affected by weather conditions, and flowering may be slower in the cold climates. Chinese Leek Flowers are sold as a premium vegetable at Oriental markets and are considered a delicacy in Oriental cooking.

  (http://www.evergreenseeds.com/chinleekflow.html).

- **Hot Pepper**—This hybrid variety produces bright green peppers that will turn into bright golden color when fully matured. Fruits are cylindrical and tapered, about 0.5" x 5" with a smooth, shiny, and thick wall. The pepper is quite pungent, has a good flavor, and is excellent for fresh and processing markets. Plants are very productive and bear lots of fruits for a long time. Plants with green and golden fruits are very beautiful and are an excellent plant for home gardening and container growing.

  (http://www.evergreenseeds.com/hotpehygohot.html).

# Description of Some Ingredients

- **Oriental (Daikon) Radish**—One of the earliest hybrids of radishes, this particular plant has extra slow bolting and uniform growing characteristics and is 12-14" long, 2-1/2" in diameter, weighs 800 grams, and has a nice straight shape. The white and fine texture of the flesh is very good for cooking, pickling, and using in salads. The plants grow very well in mild climates from early spring to summer and mature 60 days after sowing.

  (http://www.evergreenseeds.com/orradearap.html).

- **Oriental Sweet Basil, Purple Crown**—This herb is a standard version of Thai Sweet Basil and is widely grown in southern Asian countries. The plants have dark green leaves, purple stems, tips, and flowers. Young leaves and tips are harvested for cooking uses, adding flavor to various foods and soups. Plants will continue to grow more side branches and leaves for a long time.
  (http://www.evergreenseeds.com/thaibasil.html).

- **Watermelon (Hybrid Asian Sweet)**—This hybrid watermelon was developed recently by a leading seed company in Taiwan, site of the leading watermelon breeding technology center in Asia. Plants are very vigorous, widely adapted to various soil and weather conditions, and a high resistance to Fusarium wilt. The fruits are uniform, short oblong in shape, and weighing 4-5 Kgt. The green rind with dark green stripes is thin but tough which is good for storage and shipping. The bright red flesh is very juicy and sweet, with the sugar content at 12%. This high quality watermelon is very popular in Asia and widely grown for commercial use. (http://www.evergreenseeds.com/wahyassw.html)

- **Garlic**-- Although garlic may not always bring good luck, protect against evil, or ward off vampires, it is guaranteed to transform any meal into a bold, aromatic, and healthy culinary experience. Fresh, dried, and powdered garlic are available in markets throughout the year; however, fresh varieties from California are in season from June through December. Garlic comes in a head, called the "bulb," averaging about 2 inches in height and diameter and consisting of numerous small separate cloves. Both the cloves and the entire bulb are encased in paper-like sheathes that can be white, off-white, or pinkish. Although garlic cloves have a firm texture, they can be easily cut or crushed. The taste of garlic is like no other: it hits the palate with a hot pungency that is shadowed by a very subtle background sweetness. While elephant garlic has larger cloves, it is more closely related to the leek, and, therefore, does not offer the full health benefits of regular garlic.
  (http://www.whfoods.com/genpage.php)

- **Star Anise**-- Star anise is an ingredient of the traditional five-spice powder of Chinese cooking. It is also a major ingredient in the making of —pho,‖ a Vietnamese noodle soup.
  (http://en.wikipedia.org/wiki/Star_anise)

# Description of Some Ingredients

- **Ginger Roots**– Culinary use: mature ginger roots are fibrous and nearly dry. The juice from old ginger roots is extremely potent and is often used as a spice in Indian recipes and Chinese cuisine to flavor dishes such as seafood or goat meat and vegetarian cuisine.

  (http://en.wikipedia.org/wiki/Ginger )

- **Agar or Agar Agar**--This gelatinous substance is derived from seaweed. Historically and in a modern context, it is chiefly used as an ingredient in desserts throughout Japan, but in the past century it has been used extensively as a solid substrate to contain culture medium for microbiological work. The gelling agent is an un-branched polysaccharide obtained from the cell walls of some species of red algae, primarily from the genera *Gelidium* and *Gracilaria*, or seaweed (*Sphaerococcus euchema*). Commercially, it is derived primarily from *Gelidium amansii*. Agar (agar agar) can be used as a laxative, a vegetarian gelatin substitute, a thickener for soups, in jellies or ice cream, Japanese desserts, such as anmitsu, as a clarifying agent in brewing, and for paper sizing fabrics.

  (http://en.wikipedia.org/wiki/Agar)

- **Bean Threads or Cellophane noodles**--This transparent food, also known as Chinese vermicelli, bean threads, bean thread noodles, crystal noodles, or glass noodles), a type of transparent Asian noodle made from starch (such as mung bean starch, yam, potato starch, cassava or canna starch), and water. They are generally sold in the dried form, boiled to reconstitute, and then used in soups, stir fried dishes, or spring rolls. They are called cellophane noodles or "glass noodles because of their appearance. When they cooked, they resemble cellophane, a clear material or a translucent light gray or brownish-gray color. Cellophane noodles are generally round and are available in various thicknesses. Wide, flat cellophane noodle sheets called mung bean sheets are also produced in China. Cellophane noodles should not be confused with rice vermicelli, which are made from rice and white in color rather than clear.

  (http://en.wikipedia.org/wiki/Cellophane_noodles).

- **Rice Paper Wrappers**--This edible rice paper is used for making fresh summer rolls (also called spring rolls) or fried spring rolls in Vietnamese cuisine in which the rice paper is called *bánh tráng* or *bánh đa nem*. Ingredients of the food rice paper include white rice flour, tapioca flour, salt, and water. The tapioca powder makes the rice paper glutinous and smooth. It is usually sold dried in thin, crisp, translucent round sheets that are wrapped in cellophane. The sheets are dipped briefly in hot water to soften them and then wrapped around savory or sweet ingredients.

  (http://www.answers.com/topic/rice-paper).

# Description of Some Ingredients

**Rice Bits or Broken Rice--**Some rice grains break in the transport or processing of the rice from the field to the pot. Machinery is available to separate the broken grains from the whole grains. Broken rice may or may not have lower fiber and nutrient content, but generally it has an energy content similar to intact rice. The broken varieties are often less expensive, so are preferred by poorer or used as raw material (such as in beer brewing). Due to the different size and shape of the grains, broken rice has a different texture from "unbroken" rice. Some chefs and consumers may prefer the qualities of broken rice for certain dishes.

(http://en.wikipedia.org/wiki/C%C6%A1m_t%E1%BA%A5m)

**Rice Sticks or Vermicelli--**These thin noodles, sometimes also known as **rice noodles** or **rice sticks,** are made from rice. They should not be confused with cellophane noodles, which are another type of vermicelli. Rice vermicelli is a part of several Asian cuisines, in which they are often eaten as part of a soup dish, stir fry, or salads. Rice vermicelli are particularly prominent in the cuisines of the People's Republic of China, Taiwan and Southeast Asia.

(http://en.wikipedia.org/wiki/Rice_vermicelli).

**Wonton--**These bite-sized dumplings are a Chinese specialty, similar to an Italian ravioli. They consist of paper-thin dough pillows filled with a minced mixture of meat, seafood, and/or vegetables. The dough comes prepackaged as wonton skins. Wontons may be boiled, steamed. or deep-fried and served as an appetizer, snack, or side dish, usually with several sauces. They are, of course, intrinsic to wonton soup.

(http://www.answers.com/topic/wonton).

**Spring Roll Wrappers or Lumpia--**are pastries of Chinese origin similar to spring rolls popular in the Philippines and Indonesia. The recipe, both fried and fresh versions, was brought by the Chinese immigrants from the Fujian province of China to Southeast Asia and became popular where they settled in the Philippines and Indonesia. In the Netherlands and Flanders, it is spelled *loempia,* which is the old Indonesian spelling for lumpia. It has also become the generic name for "spring roll" in Dutch. A variant is the Vietnamese lumpia, it is wrapped in a thinner piece of pastry about the size of a spring roll, though the wrapping closes the ends off completely, which is typical for lumpia.
(http://en.wikipedia.org/wiki/Lumpia)

# Measurement Conversion

## Measure Equivalents

- 1 tablespoon (tbsp) = 3 teaspoons (tsp)
- 1/16 cup (c) =1 tablespoon
- 1/8 cup = 2 tablespoons
- 1/6 cup = 2 tablespoons + 2 teaspoons
- 1/4 cup = 4 tablespoons
- 1/3 cup = 5 tablespoons + 1 teaspoon
- 3/8 cup = 6 tablespoons
- 1/2 cup = 8 tablespoons
- 2/3 cup = 10 tablespoons + 2 teaspoons
- 3/4 cup = 12 tablespoons
- 1 cup = 48 teaspoons
- 1 cup= 16 tablespoons
- 8 fluid ounces (fl oz) = 1 cup
- 1 pint (pt) = 2 cups
- 1 quart (qt) = 2 pints
- 4 cups = 1 quart
- 1 gallon (gal) = 4 quarts
- 16 ounces (oz) =   1 pound (lb)
- 1 milliliter (ml) = 1 cubic centimeter (cc)
- 1 inch (in) = 2.54 centimeters (cm)

## Metric Conversion Factors

### Multiply
- Fluid Ounces *By* 29.57 *To Get* grams
- Ounces (dry) *By* 28.35 *To Get* grams
- Grams *By* 0.0353 *To Get* ounces
- Grams *By* 0.0022 *To Get* pounds
- Kilograms *By* 2.21 *To Get* pounds
- Pounds *By* 453.6 *To Get* grams
- Pounds *By* 0.4536 *To Get* kilograms
- Quarts *By* 0.946 *To Get* liters
- Quarts (dry) *By* 67.2 *To Get* cubic inches
- Quarts (liquid) *By* 57.7 *To Get* cubic inches
- Liters *By* 1.0567 *To Get* quarts
- Gallons *By* 3,785 *To Get* cubic centimeters
- Gallons *By* 3.785 *To Get* liters

(http://www.nal.usda.gov/fnic/foodcomp/Bulletins/measurement_equivalents.html)

# Nutrition Facts

## The Food Guide Pyramid--A Guide to Daily Food Choices

### Fats, Oils, & Sweets

Use these three cooking favorites sparingly. Go easy on fats and sugars, such as, butter, margarine, gravy, salad dressing, sugar, and jelly, added to foods in cooking or at the table. Choose fewer foods that are high in sugars, such as, candy, sweet desserts, and soft drinks. The most effective way to moderate the amount of fat and added sugars in your diet is to cut down on "extras" (foods in this group). Choose foods with lower fats and lower sugar foods from the other five food groups.

### Milk, Yogurt, & Cheese (2-3 Servings)

Choose skim milk and nonfat yogurt often. They are lowest in fat. One and a half to 2 ounces of cheese and 8 ounces of yogurt count as a serving from this group because they supply the same amount of calcium as 1 cup of milk. Choose "part skim" or low fat cheeses when available and lower fat milk desserts, like ice milk or frozen yogurt. Read the labels.

### Meat, Poultry, Fish (2-3 Servings)

Choose lean meat, poultry without skin, fish, and dry beans and peas often. They are the choices lowest in fat. Prepare meats in the following low fat ways:

- Trim away all the fat you can see.
- Remove skin from poultry.
- Broil, roast, or boil these foods instead of frying them.

Nuts and seeds are high in fat, so eat them in moderation.

(http://www.nal.usda.gov/fnic/Fpyr/pmap.htm)

13

# Nutrition Facts

## Vegetable Group (3-5 Servings)

Different types of vegetables provide different nutrients. Eat a variety. Include dark-green leafy vegetables and legumes several times a week in your meals, for they are especially good sources of vitamins and minerals. Legumes also provide protein and can be used in place of meat. Go easy on the fat that you add to vegetables at the table or during cooking. Added spreads or toppings, such as butter, mayonnaise, and salad dressing, count as fat.

## Fruit Group (2-4 Servings)

Choose fresh fruits, fruit juices, and frozen, canned, or dried fruit. Go easy on fruits canned or frozen in heavy syrups and sweetened fruit juices. Eat whole fruits often as they are higher in fiber than fruit juices. Count only 100 percent fruit juice as fruit. Punches, ades, and most fruit "drinks" contain only a little juice and lots of added sugars.

## Bread, Cereal, Rice, & Pasta Group (6-11 Servings)

To get the fiber you need, choose several servings a day of foods made from whole grains. Choose most often foods that are made with little fat or sugars, like bread, English muffins, rice, and pasta. Go easy on the fat and sugars that you add as spreads, seasonings, or toppings. When preparing pasta, stuffing, and sauce from packaged mixes, use only half the butter or margarine suggested; if milk or cream is called for, use low fat milk.

## What Counts as One Serving?

If you eat a larger portion, count it as more than 1 serving. For example, a dinner portion of spaghetti would count as 2 or 3 servings of pasta. Be sure to eat at least the lowest number of servings from the five major food groups listed below. You need them for the vitamins, minerals, carbohydrates, and protein they provide. Just try to pick the lowest fat choices from the food groups. No specific serving size is given for the fats, oils, and sweets group because the message is USE SPARINGLY.

(http://www.nal.usda.gov/fnic/Fpyr/pmap.htm)

# Contents

# Contents

# OTHER INGREDIENTS

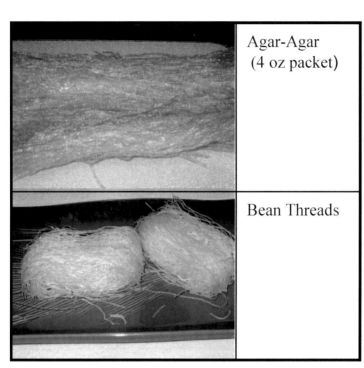

| | |
|---|---|
| | Agar-Agar (4 oz packet) |
| | Bean Threads |

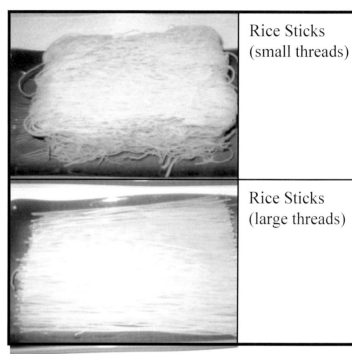

| | |
|---|---|
| | Rice Sticks (small threads) |
| | Rice Sticks (large threads) |

| | |
|---|---|
| | Vietnamese Rice Wrappers |
| | Rice Bits/Broken Rice |

| | |
|---|---|
| | Wonton Wrappers |
| | Lumpia/Spring Rolls Wrappers |

# Appetizers

- Cabbage Chicken Salad
- Summer Rolls
- Boiled Wonton Pork Dumplings
- Ground Beef in Sesame Leaves
- Stuffed Pastry Shells with Ground Pork
- Vietnamese Spring Rolls
- Papaya with Beef Jerky
- Papaya with Pork Ham and Shrimp

# Cooking Influence

**Spices and Ingredients**

Although fish sauce is traditionally used for flavoring and dipping for most Vietnamese Americans, for most of my dishes, I use soy sauce as both flavoring and dipping. In cooking, I use salt to replace fish sauce and use sugar to replace monosodium glutamate (MSG). Peanuts are also widely used in my kitchen, and a normal meal must include cooked rice.

**Style of Cooking**

Most of my dishes are stir-fried or boiled, and cooking oil is used minimally. Total cooking time is varied and can range from 30 minutes to 1 hour. Vegetables are cooked in a manner that will preserve the freshness and natural taste as much as possible. Salads and fresh cucumbers are common side dishes for each meal. Servings are approximate based on my family's eating habits and preferences. Liquid cup is used to measure both solid and liquid ingredients.

**Regional Cooking Influence**

Most of my dishes are a combination of a variety of vegetables, herbs and meats. Common herbs may include bay leaves, mint, fish mint leaves, cilantro, and perilla. Popular meats are pork, chicken, shrimp and various kinds of fish. Unlike traditional Vietnamese Americans, I use yellow onions for cooking in place of garlic. Vietnamese Americans cook differently based on their family background origins (North Vietnamese, Central Vietnamese, and South Vietnamese). A Southern Vietnamese American and influenced by my own family traditions for generations, I prefer sweet tastes and use sugar, coconut milk and toss in hot chili peppers to heat up the dishes. Simple cooking methods and using less oil are my day-to-day guide.

# Cabbage Chicken Salad

## INGREDIENTS (4 – 5 Servings)

- ½ whole fresh cabbage (rinsed, drained and shredded)
- 2 lbs. chicken breasts (1/2 whole chicken)
- fish mint leaves (diced and leave some in whole)
- 1 sweet white onion (sliced)
- *Boiling Ingredients*: 4 slices fresh ginger root, 1 yellow onion, 6 cups water and ½ tablespoon salt
- *Lime Salad Dressing*: 2 fresh limes (medium-size); ¼ cup sugar and ½ teaspoon salt

## DIRECTIONS

1. Bring the boiling ingredients (water, ginger root, onion, and salt) to a boil over medium-high heat. Add chicken to the boiling water. Bring to a boil again and reduce the heat to medium. Cover and cook for 15-20 minutes or until tender. Drain and cool. Cut chicken into bite-size pieces.
2. Make salad dressing: Combine the limes, sugar and salt in a bowl and mix well until sugar dissolves.
3. Combine the shredded cabbage with bite-size chicken pieces, diced fish mint leaves, white onion slices, and lime salad dressing and mix well.

4. Add the remaining bite-size chicken pieces into the cabbage bowl and add the remaining onion slices. Garnish with the fish mint leaves and let stand 10 minutes before serving.
5. Serve. Eat with shrimp snacks.

Note: Eat as appetizer or as a meal with chicken rice soup. Dip in salt and chili pepper paste. As an appetizer, you may add ground, unsalted roasted peanuts.

# Summer Rolls

**INGREDIENTS (Make 12 Rolls or 4 Servings)**

- 24 fresh shrimp (rinsed and drained), ¼ lb lean fresh pork ham (rinsed; drained)
- ½ small bunch of young Chinese leeks (shown)
- ¼ packet rice stick/vermicelli (thin threads)
- 1 fresh cucumber (sliced), 12 Vietnamese rice wrappers
- Hoisin sauce mix for dip
- *Boiling Ingredients:* 6 cups water, 1 teaspoon salt, 1 teaspoon sugar, 4 slices ginger root and 1 yellow onion
- *Vegetables & Herbs*: ½ small bunch Romaine lettuce, ¼ lb bean sprouts, 24 fresh mint leaves and 24 perilla leaves

**DIRECTIONS**

Bring the boiling ingredients (water, salt, sugar, and ginger root) to a boil over medium-high heat. Place the fresh pork ham into the boiling water and bring to a boil again. Reduce the heat to medium. Cover and cook for 15 minutes or until the meat is tender. Remove the pork from the pot, drain and cool.

Using the same pot and water, bring the water to a boil again over medium-high heat. Place the shrimp into the boiling water and bring it to a boil again. Cook over medium-high heat for 3 minutes or until the color changes. Remove the shrimp, drain and cool. Remove the shrimp shells and devein. Cut each shrimp in ½ and set aside.

Cut the cooked pork ham into thinly slices and set aside.

Cook the vermicelli (instructions on packet), drain and set aside.

Wet each rice wrapper in warm water and immediately, place each wrapper on a flat surface. Place 4 of the ½ cooked shrimp in the center of the rice wrapper. Add a few slices of the cooked pork ham, cooked vermicelli, 1 Romaine lettuce leaf, a few mint leaves, a few perilla leaves and some fresh bean sprouts. —Stack‖ them near the center and about 1/3 from the top of the wrapper. Fold the left and the right edges of the rice wrapper to the center. Fold the top of the wrapper over the two edges. Place a stalk of young Chinese leek over the edges (optional). Roll tightly.

Serve with Hoisin sauce mix. Add ground, unsalted roasted peanuts and hot peppers to taste.

# Boiled Wonton Pork Dumplings

## INGREDIENTS (Make 70 Pieces or 6 Servings)

- 1 lb lean fresh ground pork
- 1 packet of Wonton Wrappers (100 pieces)
- 2 tablespoons olive oil
- *Filling:* 1 whole egg, 1 roll of bean threads (soaked, diced), 1 stalk of celery (diced), 2 carrots (diced), 1 yellow onion (diced), 1 tablespoon salt, 2 tablespoons sugar and ½ teaspoon black pepper

## INSTRUCTIONS

1. Prepare the meat mixture: Combine the fresh ground pork and the filling (egg, soaked bean threads, diced celery, diced carrots, diced yellow onions, salt, sugar, and black pepper). Mix well and let stand an hour.

2. Scoop 1 tablespoon of the meat mixture and place in the center of each wrapper. Moisten edges with water and fold the wrapper in ½. Using index finger and thumb, bring the two opposite edges together, press hard and pinch edges to seal. Repeat the procedure.

3. Pour warm water into a medium-sized pot half-full and bring water to a boil over medium-high heat. Add 2 tablespoons olive oil to the boiling water to keep dumplings separate. Bring the water to a boil again. Place 15 dumplings at a time into the water. Cover and cook for 4-5 minutes or until the dumplings rise to the surface. Remove the cooked dumplings from pot and drain. Repeat the same procedure until all the dumplings are done.

4. Transfer the boiled dumplings to a serving plate.

5. Serve. Dip in Hoisin sauce or soy sauce and add hot chili paste (optional).

Note: To make the wonton soup, use chicken broth. Add an equal amount of water to the amount of the chicken broth. Mix well and bring to a boil. Place the boiled wontons into the chicken broth pot. Transfer the cooked wonton soup to a serving soup bowl. Add diced green onions, diced cilantro, and some black pepper to taste.

# Stuffed Pastry Shells with Ground Pork

**INGREDIENTS (Make 36 Pastries or 7- 8 Servings)**

- 1.5 lbs lean fresh ground pork
- 2 teaspoons corn starch
- 3 of 12 ready-to-bake puff pastry shells (round)
- 1 fresh carrot (diced), 1 yellow onion (diced) and ¼ cup green peas
- *Seasoning Mixture*: 1 tablespoon salt, 2 tablespoons sugar, ¼ teaspoon black pepper
- *Sealing Mixture*: 6 egg yolks, 1 tablespoon olive oil and ½ tablespoon sugar

## DIRECTIONS

Bake the pastry shells in the oven (instructions on packet). Cool. Using a table knife, remove the —top‖ and the soft pastry underneath. Set aside.

Place the ground pork into a large pan and cook over medium-high heat, stirring constantly until the meat is separated and turns a golden brown. Remove excess oil and transfer the cooked ground pork to a bowl.

Make the meat mixture: Using the same pan, add diced onions and stir for 1 minute over medium-high heat. Pour the cooked ground pork back into the pan, then the diced carrots and the green peas. Add the seasoning mixture (salt, sugar and black pepper) to the pan, stirring until blended. Cook for 8 minutes over medium-high heat. Reduce the heat to medium and add 2 teaspoons corn starch to pan. Stir well and remove the cooked meat mixture from heat.

Make the egg yolk sealing mixture: Combine egg yolks, olive oil, and sugar and mix well to eliminate any lumps. Set aside.

Fill each pastry shell with 2 tablespoons of the cooked meat mixture through the —top‖. Press firmly and put the —top‖ back into each pastry shell to close. Using a small brush, spread the egg yolk sealing mixture around the edge and the top of each pastry shell to close. Place the stuffed pastry shells back into the oven at 275 degrees. Bake for 10 minutes or until the top of each pastry shell turns a golden brown.

Serve warm. Eat with Tabasco red pepper sauce (optional)

# Vietnamese Spring Rolls

**INGREDIENTS (Make 50 Rolls or 8 Servings)**

- 2.5 lbs fresh ground pork
- 2 packets spring roll wrappers/lumpia (25 pieces in a bag, or cut each in ½ to make 50 rolls)
- Cooking oil for deep fry
- 2 egg whites (whisk gently)
- *Filling*: 1.5 lbs fresh carrots (shredded), 2 yellow onions (diced), 1 roll of bean threads (soaked in warm water, rinsed, drained and diced), 2 whole eggs, 2 tablespoons salt, 4 tablespoons sugar and ½ teaspoon black pepper

**DIRECTIONS**

1. Make the meat mixture: In a large bowl, combine the fresh ground pork and the filling (salt, sugar, black pepper, shredded carrots, diced onions, diced bean threads, and eggs). Mix thoroughly and let stand 1 hour.

2. Place each spring roll wrapper on a flat surface. Scoop 2 tablespoons of the meat mixture and place it into the center of each wrapper, near the center and about 1/3 from top. Fold the left and the right edges of the wrapper to the center. Fold the top of the wrapper over the two edges. Roll tightly. Seal the roll with egg whites. Repeat the same procedure.

3. Pour the cooking oil into a deep fryer half-full and preheat at 375 degrees. Meanwhile, put as many rolls as possible into the basket of the deep fryer. Place them tightly to each other to prevent the rolls from separating while cooking. Place the uncooked spring roll basket into the hot oil. Cover and cook in the deep fryer for 12 minutes or until golden brown. When the rolls turn a golden brown, remove the cooked spring rolls from deep fryer and transfer to paper towels to drain, then to a serving plate.

4. Serve warm. Garnish with the fish mint leaves or any herbs of your choice. Eat by alone, with lettuce and cucumbers, and/or dip in the fish sauce mix.

# Papaya with Beef Jerky

**INGREDIENTS (2 Servings)**

- ½ lb shredded green papaya (rinsed with cold water and drained)
- ½ cup Beef Jerky (cut in thinly strips)
- 6 Asian bay leaves (sliced)
- *Lime Juice Dressing (Make ¼ cup)*: 1 whole lime, 3 ½ tablespoons sugar, 1 tablespoon all-purpose soy sauce and ½ tablespoon hot chili sauce

**DIRECTIONS**

1. Make the lime juice dressing: Combine the lime, sugar, soy sauce, and hot chili sauce and mix well until sugar dissolves. Set aside.
2. Place the shredded green papaya onto a serving plate.
3. Top with the beef jerky strips and the bay leave slices.
4. Pour about ½ the amount of the lime juice dressing over the papaya.
5. Serve. Add the remaining of the lime juice dressing over the shredded papaya and/or additional beef jerky to your liking.

Note: Green papaya and shredded green papaya can be found in the vegetable section of most Asian grocery stores. Ripe papaya is a fruit and can be found in the fruit section. Also, you may substitute mint leaves for bay leaves.

# Ground Beef in Sesame Leaves

**INGREDIENTS (2 – 3 Servings)**
- 40 fresh large sesame leaves (rinsed and drained)
- ½ lb lean ground beef
- *Filling:* ½ roll bean threads (soaked in warm water, diced), 1 yellow onion (diced), 1 fresh carrot (diced), 1 teaspoon salt, 2 teaspoons sugar, ¼ teaspoon black pepper, 1 whole egg
- *Oil Mixture:* 2 tablespoons olive oil, 1 stalk green onion (use the white portion, diced)

**INSTRUCTIONS**

1. Make the meat mixture: Combine the ground beef and the filling (diced yellow onions, diced carrots, soaked bean threads, salt, sugar, black pepper, and egg). Mix well and let stand 30 minutes.

2. Make the sesame rolls: Place each sesame leaf on a flat surface. Scoop ½ tablespoon of the meat mixture and place it in the center of leaf. Fold the left and the right edges to the center of leaf. Fold the top leaf into the center and over the left and the right edges of leaf. Repeat the procedure.

3. Preheat the oven to 375 degrees.

4. Using a brush, coat baking tray with the olive oil or spray with cooking spray. Place the rolls into the baking tray and sprinkle some olive oil over the rolls to prevent dryness while cooking. Cook for 30 minutes or until the meat is well done. Remove from the oven and transfer the cooked rolls to a serving plate.

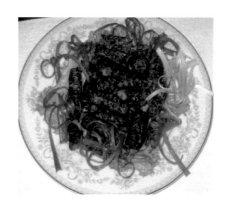

5. Make the oil mixture: Pour 2 tablespoons olive oil into a microwavable bowl. Cook in the microwave for 2 minutes or until the oil is hot. Remove from the microwave and add diced green onions. Pour oil mixture over the cooked rolls (optional).

6. Serve. Dip in soy sauce or Hoisin sauce mix.

   Note: Eat as appetizer or as a meal. To serve as an appetizer, add ground unsalted, roasted peanuts. As a meal, eat with cooked rice sticks/vermicelli and Hoisin sauce mix.

# Papaya with Pork Ham& Shrimp

## INGREDIENTS (4 Servings)
- 1 lb shredded green papaya (rinsed and drained)
- ½ lb lean fresh pork ham (rinsed and drained)
- 16 whole shrimp (medium or large, rinsed and drained)
- 6 bay leaves (diced)
- *Lime Juice Dressing*: 1 whole lime, 3 ½tablespoons sugar and ½ teaspoon salt
- *Boiling Ingredients*: 5 cups water, 1 yellow onion, 4 slices fresh ginger root, 1 teaspoon salt and 1 teaspoon sugar

## DIRECTIONS

Bring the boiling ingredients (water, ginger root, onion, salt, and sugar) to a boil over medium-high heat. Place the pork ham into the boiling water and bring to a boil again. Reduce the heat to medium, cover and cook for 15 to 20 minutes or until tender. Remove the cooked pork from pot. Drain and let cool. Discard excess fat that may rise to the surface. Cut cooked pork ham into very thin slices.

Using the same pot and water, bring the water to a boil again over medium-high heat. Place the shrimp into the boiling water and bring it to a boil again. Cook for 3 minutes or until the color of the shrimp changes to red. Remove the shrimp from the pot and immediately rinse with cold water. Drain, remove the shells and devein.

Make the lime juice dressing: Combine the lime juice, sugar, and salt and mix well until the sugar dissolves.

Place the shredded green papaya onto a large serving plate and add the cooked pork ham slices and the cooked shrimp. Pour the lime juice dressing over the shredded papaya and mix well. Top with the diced bay leaves, the remaining cooked ham and shrimp. Add additional lime juice dressing to your liking.

Serve. Eat by itself, with bread or with a main course.

Note: Leftovers can be placed in the refrigerator for next day use. You may substitute mint leaves for bay leaves.

# Soups & Salads

- Chicken Rice Soup
- Bean Threads Soup
- Crabmeat & Asparagus Soup
- Ground Beef & Rice Soup
- Herb Salad
- Home-Styled Salad
- Summer Salad

# Chicken Rice Soup

## INGREDIENTS (5 - 6 Servings)

- 2 lbs chicken breasts
- 1/3 cup long-grain rice (rinsed and drained)
- 1 stalk of green onion (diced)
- Few stems of fresh cilantro (diced)
- Freshly ground black pepper to taste
- *Boiling Ingredients*: 6 cups water, 2 teaspoons salt, 1 teaspoon sugar, 4 slices fresh ginger root and 1 yellow onion

## DIRECTIONS

Bring the boiling ingredients (water, salt, sugar, ginger root, and yellow onion) to a boil over medium-high heat. Place the chicken breasts into the boiling water, bring to a boil again and reduce the heat to medium. Cover and cook for 10 to 12 minutes or until tender. If using the whole chicken, turn the chicken over to the other side and cook for additional 10 minutes. Remove the chicken from the pot and let it cool. Let the broth simmer and skim any fat that rises to the surface. Discard the cooked ginger root slices and the onion. Save the broth to cook the long-grain rice.

Cut the cooked chicken breasts into bite-size pieces and set aside (reserve some chicken slices to make the cabbage chicken salad if desired).

Use the same pot and the broth, place the long-grain rice into the pot, bring to a boil over medium-high heat and reduce the heat to low-medium. Cover and simmer for 30 minutes or until the kernels are open, stirring occasionally. Transfer the rice soup to a serving bowl.

Serve warm. Top with the cooked chicken pieces, diced green onions and cilantro and freshly ground black pepper.

Note: You may substitute 1 whole chicken for chicken breasts. For fast cooking, use 3 cups of cooked rice instead.

# Bean Threads Soup

## INGREDIENTS (1 Serving)

- 1 roll (2 oz) dry bean threads
- 1 can (14 oz) chicken broth
- 1 stalk green onion (diced)
- 2 stems fresh cilantro (diced)
- ¼ teaspoon black pepper

## INSTRUCTIONS

1. Soak the bean threads in warm water for 5 minutes or until soft. Cut into bite-size strips and drain.

2. Pour the broth into a microwavable bowl and cook in the microwave for 5 minutes. Remove the bowl from the microwave. Add the bean threads and cover for 1 minute.

3. Add the diced green onions, diced fresh cilantro to the soup bowl and mix well. Add black pepper to taste.

4. Serve warm.

Note: Ideal for a quick lunch!

# Crabmeat and Asparagus Soup

## INGREDIENTS (2 Servings)

- 1 can (15 oz) white Asparagus (peeled)
- 1 can (14 oz) chicken broth, 14 oz water
- 1 egg white, 1 teaspoon olive oil
- 1 yellow onion, 1 stalk of celery (cut in ½)
- ½ cup crabmeat, ½ teaspoon salt, ¼ teaspoon black pepper
- 2 stems cilantro (diced)
- *Thickening Mixture*: 2 tablespoons corn starch and 4 tablespoons water

## INSTRUCTIONS

1. Combine the crab meat, ½ teaspoon salt and ¼ teaspoon black pepper. Mix well and let stand 5 minutes.

2. Place the crabmeat into a medium-sized pan, stirring well to separate the crabmeat over medium-high heat for 3 minutes. Carefully remove all remaining crab shells that are still attached and set aside.

3. Combine the chicken broth and water, 14oz each. Add the yellow onion and the celery to pot and bring to a boil over medium-high heat. Reduce the heat to medium, cover and cook for 15 minutes. Discard the cooked onion and celery.

4. Combine the egg white and 1 teaspoon olive oil and mix well. Slowly pour the egg white mixture into pot, stirring constantly until blended. Pour the cooked crabmeat back into the pot.

5. Prepare the thickening mixture: combine the corn starch and the water and mix well to eliminate any lumps.

6. Slowly pour the thickening mixture into the soup pot, stirring constantly over low-medium heat until the broth is clear. Place the Asparagus into pot, stirring gently. Bring to a boil again and turn off the heat. Transfer the soup to a serving bowl. Top with diced cilantro and black pepper.

7. Serve warm.

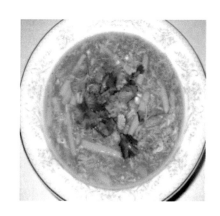

# Ground Beef & Rice Soup

## INGREDIENTS ( 4 Servings)

- ½ cup uncooked long-grain Jasmine rice (rinsed and drained)
- 7 cups water
- 10 oz lean ground beef
- 1 yellow onion (diced)
- 1 stalk of green onion (diced)
- 2 stems cilantro (diced)
- *Seasoning Ingredients*: ½ teaspoon salt, ½ teaspoon sugar and ¼ teaspoon black pepper

## INSTRUCTIONS

1. In a medium-sized pot, bring 7 cups water and the long-grain rice to a boil over high heat. Reduce the heat to medium. Cover and cook for about 30 minutes or until the kernels are open, stirring occasionally. Reduce the heat to low.

2. Place the ground beef into a pan and stir well, to separate the meat, over medium-high heat for 10 minutes or until golden brown. Reduce the heat to medium. Remove excess fat that rises to the surface. Add the diced onions and the seasoning ingredients (salt, sugar and black pepper) to the pan, stirring thoroughly until blended. Turn off the heat.

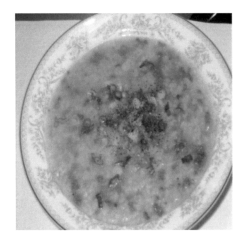

3. Pour the cooked ground beef back into the rice soup pot. Turn the heat to low-medium. Cover and cook for 10 minutes, stirring occasionally. Remove excess fat that rises to the surface. Turn off the heat.

4. Transfer the cooked rice and ground beef soup to a serving bowl. Top with the diced green onions and cilantro and black pepper.

5. Serve. Add additional salt and black pepper as needed.

# Herb Salad

## INGREDIENTS (2 Servings)

- 2 fresh cucumbers (rinsed, drained and thinly sliced)
- 2 fresh carrots (rinsed, drained and thinly cut)
- 10 (regular) mint leaves
- 1 small bunch of fish mint leaves
- 1 small bunch of perilla leaves (tia-to)
- *Lime Salad Dressing (to make ¼ cup)*: ½ whole lime, 1 ½ tablespoons sugar and 1 teaspoon salt

## DIRECTIONS

Make the salad dressing: Combine the lime, sugar and salt and mix well until sugar dissolves. Set aside.

Place the regular and fish mint leaves, the perilla (tia-to), the cucumber slices and the thinly cut carrots into a serving bowl.

Pour the salad dressing over the salad and mix lightly. Let stand 5 minutes. Add additional salad dressing to your liking.

Serve

Note: This salad dish is great with barbecue meat, fish or with any seafood dish.

# Home-Styled Salad

**INGREDIENTS (2 Servings)**

- 2 fresh cucumbers (rinsed, drained and thinly sliced)
- ½ bunch red leave lettuce (rinsed, drained and cut)
- 1 red bell pepper (rinsed, drained and thinly sliced)
- 1 white sweet onion (thinly sliced)
- *Lime Salad Dressing (to make ¼ cup)*: ½ lime, 1 ½ tablespoons sugar, and 1 teaspoon salt

**DIRECTIONS**

1. Arrange cucumbers, red bell peppers, sweet white onions, and red leave lettuce in a large serving plate.
2. Make the salad dressing: Combine the lime, sugar and salt and mix well until sugar dissolves.
3. Pour the salad dressing over the salad and toss lightly. Let stand 5 minutes.
4. Serve. Eat as a side dish or with any meat dish. Note: photo on the right shows a 4-serving salad plate. You may substitute the vinegar salad dressing for the lime salad dressing. To make ¾ *cup*: Combine ¼ cup apple cider vinegar, ¼ cup water, ½ cup sugar, ½ teaspoon salt, ½ teaspoon olive oil and ¼ teaspoon black pepper and mix well.

# Summer Salad

**INGREDIENTS ( 2 Servings)**

- 2 fresh cucumbers (rinsed, drained, cut in ½ and thinly sliced)
- 2 large tomatoes (rinsed, drained, cut in ½ and thinly sliced)
- ½ bunch Romaine lettuce (rinsed, drained and cut into bite-size portions)
- 1 sweet white onion (cut in ½ and thinly sliced)
- *Lime Salad Dressing (to make ¼ cup)*: ½lime, 1 ½ tablespoons sugar, and 1 teaspoon salt

**DIRECTIONS**

Place the Romaine lettuce leaves, onion slices, cucumber slices and tomato slices into a salad bowl.

Make the salad dressing: Combine the lime, sugar and salt and mix well until sugar dissolves. Let stand 5 minutes.

Pour the salad dressing over the salad.

Serve. Eat as a side dish or with any meat dish.

Note: You may substitute the vinegar salad dressing for the lime salad dressing. To make ¾ cup: Combine ¼ cup apple cider vinegar, ¼ cup water, ½ cup sugar, ½ teaspoon salt, ½ teaspoon olive oil and ½ teaspoon black pepper and mix well.

# Salad Dressings & Dips

- Vinegar Salad Dressing
- Fish Sauce Mix
- Hoisin Sauce Mix

# Vinegar Salad Dressing

**INGREDIENTS (One ¾ cup Serving)**

- ¼ cup apple cider vinegar
- ¼ cup water (warm water), ½ cup sugar
- ½ teaspoon salt
- ½ teaspoon olive oil
- ¼ teaspoon black pepper (optional)
- One white sweet onion (cut into rings)

**DIRECTIONS**

In a bowl, combine ½ cup sugar and ¼ cup warm water in a bowl and mix well until sugar dissolves. Add ¼ cup vinegar, ½ teaspoon salt, ½ teaspoon olive oil and ¼ teaspoon black pepper. Mix well.

Cut white onions into rings and add them to vinegar salad dressing bowl

Place in the refrigerator to chill until ready-to-serve

Note: You may substitute the lime salad dressing for the vinegar salad dressing. To make ¼ cup: combine ½ whole lime, 1 ½ tablespoons sugar and 1 teaspoon salt and mix well.

# Fish Sauce Mix

**INGREDIENTS (Make 1 ¾ cups)**

- ¼ cup apple cider vinegar
- ½ cup sugar
- ½ cup warm water
- ½ cup fish sauce
- 1 teaspoon ground fresh chili paste

**DIRECTIONS**

1. In a bowl, combine ½ cup warm water and ½ cup sugar and mix well until sugar dissolves. Add ¼ cup apple cider vinegar. Add ½ cup fish sauce. Add 1 teaspoon ground fresh chili paste. Mix thoroughly.

2. Serve over rice, meat dishes and rice sticks/vermicelli.

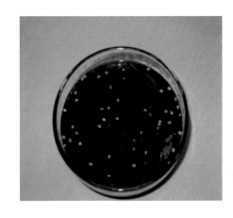

# Hoisin Sauce Mix

## INGREDIENTS ( 3 Servings)

- 3 tablespoons Hoisin sauce
- 3 tablespoons water (warm)
- 3 ½ tablespoons sugar
- 1 tablespoon apple cider vinegar
- ½ teaspoon ground fresh chili paste
- 2 tablespoons unsalted roasted peanuts (ground)
- 3 fresh hot chili pepper (optional)

## INSTRUCTIONS

In a bowl, combine 3 ½ tablespoons sugar and 3 tablespoons warm water and mix well until sugar dissolves. Add 3 tablespoons Hoisin sauce, 1 tablespoon apple cider and ½ teaspoon ground fresh chili paste. Mix well until blended.

Top with ground unsalted roasted peanuts.

Garnish with fresh hot chili peppers.

Place in the refrigerator to chill until ready-to-serve (optional)

# Main Courses

Barbecue Pork Ribs

Stir-Fried Linguine & Beef Steaks

Linguine with Stuffed Tomatoes & Ground Beef

Barbecue Pork Sirloins & Peanuts

Chicken Stew in Tomato Paste

Shrimp with Onions & Hot Peppers

Salt & Pepper Crabs

Squid with Green Onions & Hot Peppers

Lobster with Ginger and Onions

Lobster in Onions

Ox Tail Soup (Vietnamese PHO)

Boiled Egg Noodles & Seafood

Boiled Chicken with Rice in Chicken Broth

Barbecue Pork Ribs & Broken Rice

Shredded Pork Ham with Rice Sticks & Coconut Milk

Stir-Fried Tofu & Vegetables

Shredded Pork Ham

Shredded Pork Ham with Rice Sticks & Peanuts

Barbecue Pork with Rice Sticks & Spring Rolls

Fresh Pork Ham in Coconut Soda

Mixed Vegetables & Shrimp

Stir-fried Shrimp with Vegetables

Sweet Rice & Chinese Sausages

Fish & Herbs in Soy Sauce

Shrimp Fried Rice

Roast Duck

Beef Stew with Carrots

# Barbecue Pork Ribs

**INGREDIENTS (5 Servings)**
- 4 lbs pork ribs (rinsed, drained and cut in 1 ½-inch thick pieces)
- 1 yellow onion (diced)
- 2 tablespoons red wine or any cooking rice wine (optional)
- *Barbecue Ingredients*: 1 teaspoon ground black pepper, ½ cup all-purpose soy sauce, 2 tablespoons Hoisin sauce and 1/3 cup sugar

**DIRECTIONS**

Make the barbecue sauce: Combine the barbecue ingredients (black pepper, soy sauce, Hoisin sauce and sugar) in a bowl and mix well until sugar dissolves.

Combine the pork ribs, diced onions and the barbecue sauce and mix well. Turn the ribs to the other side until all sides are coated with the barbecue sauce evenly. Let stand 3 hours.

Preheat a grill to high or place a grill pan over high heat. Oil the grill or the pan. Grill the ribs, 8 to 10 minutes per side, turning occasionally and basting with the barbecue sauce on both sides, and grill until golden brown. Transfer the cooked ribs from the grill to a serving plate. Repeat the same procedure until all the ribs are grilled.

Garnish with the fish mint leaves and the perilla (tia-to) leaves.

Serve with steamed rice, fish sauce mix and salad of your choice; or eat with bread and salad of your choice.

Note: you may substitute all-purpose soy sauce for fish sauce mix

# Stir-Fried Linguine & Beef Steaks

**INGREDIENTS (2 Servings)**

- 8 oz linguine
- 1 lb round bottom round steak (cut in ½ and tenderized)
- ½ teaspoon salt, ¼ teaspoon black pepper
- 2 tablespoons olive oil
- 1 yellow onion (sliced)
- Boston lettuce, 1 cucumber (sliced) and 1 tomato (sliced)

**INSTRUCTIONS**

1. Cook the linguine (instructions on packet). Rinse with cold water and drain.

2. Rub both sides of the round steaks with ½ teaspoon salt and ¼ teaspoon black pepper. Let stand 5 minutes.

3. Heat 2 tablespoons olive oil in a large pan over high heat for 3 minutes or until oil is hot, but not smoking. Place the steaks into the pan and fry for 3 minutes over high heat or until golden brown. Turn to the other side and continue to fry for another 3 minutes until meat turns brown evenly. Turn off the heat and transfer the steaks to a serving plate. Discard excess oil.

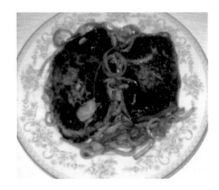

4. Using the same pan, place the onion slices into the pan, stirring over medium-high heat for 1 minute or until the color of the onions changes. Turn off the heat. Transfer the fried onion slices to the steak plate (top photo). Discard the remaining excess oil.

5. Prepare the fried linguine: Using the same pan, preheat the pan for 2 minutes over medium-high heat. Place the cooked linguine into the pan and toss well over medium-high heat for 3 minutes. Turn off the heat and transfer the fried linguine to a serving plate.

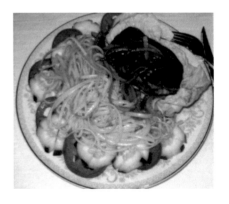

6. Serve warm. Eat with Boston lettuce leaves, cucumbers, and tomatoes or salad of your choice, soy sauce, and hot chili paste.

# Linguine with Stuffed Tomatoes & Ground Beef

## INGREDIENTS (4 Servings)

- *Beef Mixture Ingredients*: 1.20 lbs lean ground beef, 3 teaspoons salt, 1 ½ tablespoons sugar, ½ teaspoon black pepper, 1 egg, 1 roll (2 oz) bean threads (soaked, drained and diced) and 1 yellow onion (diced)
- 7 fresh large tomatoes (cut in ½ crosswise)
- 8 oz linguine
- ½ cup cooking oil
- green onions and cilantro (see photo)

## INSTRUCTIONS

1. Cook the linguine (instructions on packet). Rinse with cold water and drain.
2. Combine the ground beef mixture ingredients (ground beef, salt, sugar, black pepper, egg, soaked bean threads, diced yellow onions) and mix well. Let stand 30 minutes.
3. Remove seeds from the tomatoes. Fill each tomato with approximately 2 tablespoons of the ground beef mixture. Press firmly and set aside.
4. Heat ½ cup cooking oil in a large pan over medium-high heat for 3 minutes or until the oil is hot. Place the stuffed tomatoes into the hot oil. Cook for 8 to 10 minutes per side, turning once. Check occasionally to make sure that the tomatoes are not mushy. Remove the cooked stuffed tomatoes to a serving plate. Continue to cook until all the stuffed tomatoes are cooked. Turn off the heat and discard excess oil.
5. Make the stir-fried linguine: Using the same pan, preheat the pan over high heat for 2 minutes. Pour the cooked linguine into the hot pan and stir well for 2 to 3 minutes. Transfer the fried linguine from pan to a serving plate.
6. Serve. Eat with salad of your choice, soy sauce and hot chili pepper.

Note: you may substitute steamed rice or spaghetti for the linguine.

# Barbecue Pork Sirloins & Peanuts

**INGREDIENTS (5 Servings)**

- 4 lbs boneless pork sirloins (rinsed, drained and cut in 1 ½ -inch strips)
- 1 yellow onion (diced)
- ½ cup ground unsalted roasted peanuts
- Mint leaves
- *Barbecue Ingredients*: 1 teaspoons ground black pepper, ½ cup all-purpose soy sauce, 2 tablespoons Hoisin sauce and 1/3 cup sugar

**DIRECTIONS**

1. Make the barbecue sauce: Combine the barbecue ingredients (black pepper, soy sauce, Hoisin sauce, and sugar) in a bowl and mix well until sugar dissolves.

2. Combine the pork sirloin strips, diced onions, and the barbecue sauce and mix well. Turn to the other side and continue to turn occasionally until all sides are coated well. Let stand 1 hour.

3. Preheat a grill to high or place a grill pan over high heat. Oil the grill or the pan. Grill the meat, 8 to 10 minutes per side, or until golden brown, turning occasionally and basting with the barbecue sauce on both sides. Repeat the procedure, if needed.

4. Transfer the cooked pork meat to a serving plate. Top with ground unsalted roasted peanuts. Garnish with mint leaves.

5. Serve warm. Eat with steamed rice, cooked broken rice, rice sticks/vermicelli, bread and salad of your choice. Dip in soy sauce or fish sauce mix.

# Chicken Stew in Tomato Paste

**INGREDIENTS (4 Servings)**

- 3 lbs chicken breasts (rinsed, drained and cut into bite-size pieces)
- 1 yellow onion (sliced), ½ lb fresh potato (cut in ½ each), ½ lb fresh carrot (cut in ½ each)
- 1 ½ tablespoons salt, 3 tablespoons sugar, ½ teaspoon black pepper
- 2 tablespoons cooking oil
- *Tomato Paste Ingredients*: 1 teaspoon olive oil, 1 teaspoon sugar and 2 tablespoons tomato paste
- *Thickening Ingredients:* ½ tablespoon cornstarch and 2 tablespoons water

**DIRECTIONS**

1. Place the cut potatoes and carrots in a microwavable bowl and cook in the microwave for 10 minutes. Set aside.

2. Prepare the tomato paste mixture: Combine the tomato paste ingredients (olive oil, sugar and tomato paste) and mix well. Place in the microwave for 1 minute. Remove from the microwave and mix well.

3. Heat 2 tablespoons cooking oil in a pan over medium-high heat for 2 minutes. Place ½ the amount of the onion slices into the pan, stirring until golden brown. Add the chicken pieces into the pan, stirring for 5 minutes or until the color changes. Add 1 ½ tablespoons salt, 3 tablespoons sugar, ½ teaspoon black pepper and tomato paste mixture to the pan. Stir thoroughly over medium-high heat for 5 minutes or until blended. Turn off the heat.

4. Pour 6 cups water into a pot and bring to a boil over medium-high heat. Place the cooked potatoes, carrots and the cooked chicken pieces into the boiling water and stir gently. Reduce the heat to low-medium. Cover and simmer for 15 minutes or until the chicken pieces, the potatoes and carrots are tender, but not mushy.

5. Prepare the thickening sauce: Combine the thickening ingredients (cornstarch and water) and mix well to eliminate any lumps. Slowly pour the thickening sauce into the pot, stirring constantly until the broth is clear. Turn off the heat and transfer the chicken stew to a serving bowl. Add black pepper and garnish with fresh onion slices and perilla leaves.

6. Serve warm. Eat with bread or steamed rice. Add additional salt and black pepper to taste.

# Shrimp with Onions & Hot Peppers

## INGREDIENTS (2 Servings)

- 10 large-sized shrimp with/or without heads (rinsed and drained)
- 2 tablespoons shrimp batter mix
- 1 stalk green onion (cut in 3 sections)
- 1 yellow onion (sliced)
- 4 hot peppers
- ½ cup cooking oil
- *Seasoning Mixture*: ½ teaspoon salt, ½ teaspoon ground black pepper and ½ teaspoon sugar (combine, mix well and set aside)

## INSTRUCTIONS

1. Sprinkle the shrimp batter mix on both sides of the shrimp. Shake the excess flour from the shrimp.

2. Heat ½ cup cooking oil in a medium-sized pan over medium-high heat for 3 minutes. Place the shrimp one at a time into the hot pan and fry over medium-high heat for 1 minute per side, turning once. Remove the shrimp to a serving plate (top photo). Turn off the heat and remove excess oil from the pan.

3. Using the same pan, preheat the pan over medium-high heat for 2 minutes. Put the cooked shrimp back into the pan. Sprinkle the seasoning mixture (salt, black pepper and sugar) all over the shrimp and toss gently over medium-high heat for 2 minutes or until blended.

4. Place the green onions, hot peppers and the yellow onion slices into the pan, stirring well over medium-high heat for 1 minute, then to stir in with the shrimp for 1 minute. Turn off the heat and transfer the cooked shrimp to a serving plate.

5. Serve warm. Eat with cooked rice and your choice of salad as a meal.

# Salt & Pepper Crabs

## INGREDIENTS (2 Servings)

- *Flour Mixture*: ½ cup all-purpose flour, ¼ cup corn starch, 1 tablespoon salt and 1 tablespoon ground black pepper (combine, mix well and set aside)
- *Seasoning Mixture*: 3 teaspoons sugar, 3 teaspoons sea salt and
  3 teaspoons ground black pepper (combine, mix well and set aside)
- 12 large blue crabs (cleaned and cut each in ½)
- 3 stalks of green onions (cut each in 3 portions)
- 4 hot peppers (if using big hot peppers, cut each in ½)
- 2 cups cooking oil

## INSTRUCTIONS

1. Coat cut crabs with the flour mixture. Shake the excess flour from the crabs.

2. Heat 2 cups cooking oil in a large pan over high heat for about 3 minutes. Place each coated crab into the hot oil and fry for 1 minute per side. Repeat the process as needed and until the crabs look crunchy. Transfer the cooked crabs to a large serving plate. Continue the same process until all crabs are fried. Discard the excess oil.

3. Using the same pan, preheat the pan over medium-high heat for about 1 minute. Pour the cooked crabs back into the hot pan (divide into 2 portions and do 2 times if pan is not large enough to hold all of them) and immediately, sprinkle the seasoning mixture all over the cooked crabs. Keep tossing for a few minutes until all the seasoning is well combined with the cooked crabs and to keep the crabs crunchy.

4. Place the cut green onions and the hot peppers into the pan, stirring well with the cooked crabs for 1 minute. Turn off the heat and transfer the cooked crabs to the large serving plate.

5. Serve warm. Eat as a meal with steamed rice or as an appetizer.

Note: Ground white pepper is preferred for this dish!

# Squid with Green Onions & Hot Peppers

## INGREDIENTS (2 Servings)

- 2 whole squid (1 lb total, cleaned, rinsed, drained and cut into 32 pieces)
- ½ sweet white onion (sliced)
- 3 stalks green onions (cut into 6 sections)
- 4 hot peppers (if using large ones, cut each in ½)
- 4 tablespoons cooking oil
- *Seasoning Mixture*: ¼ teaspoon salt, ¼ teaspoon sugar and ¼ teaspoon black pepper (combine, mix well and set aside)
- *Flour Mixture*: 2 tablespoons all-purpose flour, 1 ½ tablespoons corn starch, ½ teaspoon salt and ½ teaspoon black pepper (combine, mix well and set aside)

## INSTRUCTIONS

1. Pat the squid with paper towels to remove excess water from the squid. Sprinkle the flour mixture over both sides of the cut squid. Remove the excess flour before cooking.

2. Heat 4 tablespoons cooking oil in a medium-sized pan over medium-high heat for 3 minutes. Immediately place the squid into the hot oil and fry for ½ to 1 minute over medium-high heat per side or until the squid color turns brown. Turn off the heat and transfer the cooked squid to a serving plate. Remove the excess oil.

3. Using the same pan, preheat the pan over medium heat for 2 minutes. Pour the cooked squid back into the hot pan and sprinkle the seasoning mixture (salt, sugar and black pepper) all over the squid. Stir well over medium heat until the seasoning is well blended.

4. Place the green onions and the hot peppers into the pan, stirring over medium heat with the squid for ½ a minute. Turn off the heat and transfer the cooked squid to a serving plate. Garnish with lettuce leaves and sweet white onion slices.

5. Serve warm. Eat with steamed rice and your choice of salad. Dip in soy sauce.

# Lobster with Ginger & Onions

## INGREDIENTS (1- 2 Servings)

- *Seasoning Mixture*: 2 teaspoons salt, 2 teaspoons sugar and ¼ teaspoon ground black pepper (combine, mix well and set aside)
- 2 lbs whole lobster (rinsed and drained)
- 4 slices fresh ginger root (thinly sliced)
- 1 stalk green onion (cut into 3 sections)
- ½ yellow onion (diced)
- fish mint leaves
- 2 tablespoons cooking oil

## DIRECTIONS

1. Pour 6 cups water into a large pot and bring to a boil over high heat. Place the lobster into the boiling water and use a skewer to keep the lobster from curling. Cook in the boiling water for 10 minutes or until the color of the lobster changes to a deep red. Remove lobster from the pot and drain.

2. Remove the lobster flesh from the tail and devein. Cut into bite-size pieces. Save the shell.

3. Heat 2 tablespoons cooking oil in a pan over medium-high heat for 3 minutes. Place the ginger and yellow onion slices into the pan and stir for 1 minute. Put the lobster flesh into the pan. Add the seasoning mixture (salt, sugar and black pepper), stirring well with the lobster flesh, ginger and onions for ½ a minute or until blended. Add the cut green onions and stir altogether for ½ a minute. Turn off the heat.

4. Transfer the cooked lobster flesh from the pan to the lobster shell and place onto a serving plate (as shown). Garnish with fish mint leaves.

5. Serve warm. Eat with steamed rice and soy sauce. Add hot chili paste (optional)

# Lobster in Onions

**INGREDIENTS (1- 2 Servings)**

- 1 (2 lbs) whole lobster (rinsed and drained)
- 2 tablespoons cooking oil
- 1 yellow onion (chopped)
- Romaine lettuce leaves
- *Seasoning Mixture*: 2 teaspoons salt, ¼ teaspoon ground black pepper and 4 teaspoons sugar (combine, mix well and set aside)

**DIRECTIONS**

1. Pour 6 cups water into a large pot and bring to a boil over high heat. Place the lobster into the boiling water and use a skewer to keep the lobster from curling. Cook in the boiling water for 10 minutes or until the color of the lobster changes to a deep red. Remove lobster from the pot and drain.

2. Remove the lobster flesh from the tail and devein. Cut into bite-size pieces. Save the shell.

3. Heat 2 tablespoons cooking oil in a pan over medium-high heat for 3 minutes. Place the chopped onions into the pan and stir for 1 minute or until the color of the onions changes to a light brown. Put the lobster flesh into the pan. Add the seasoning mixture (salt, sugar and black pepper), stirring well with the lobster flesh and onions for ½ a minute or until blended. Check the seasoning. Turn off the heat.

4. Transfer the cooked lobster flesh from the pan to the lobster shell and place onto a serving plate (as shown). Garnish with lettuce.

5. Serve warm. Eat with steamed rice and soy sauce. Add hot chili paste (optional)

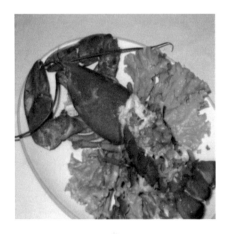

# Ox Tail Soup (Vietnamese Pho)

## INGREDIENTS (4 – 5 Servings)

- *Herb Mixture*: 3 stalks green onion (diced), 10 stems cilantro (diced), 1 sweet white onion (sliced)
- *Seasoning Ingredients*: 2 tablespoons salt, 4 ½ tablespoons sugar, 2 teaspoons MSG (optional), 10 slices ginger root, 10 dried anise seeds, 1 large yellow onion and 1 lb white Oriental radish (cut in bite-size portions)
- 3 lbs ox tails
- ½ lb fresh bean sprouts (washed and drained), bay leaves
- 1 package (16 oz) dried rice noodles
- Hot chili paste, Hoisin sauce, and black pepper to taste.

## DIRECTIONS

1. Place the anise seeds and ginger root slices into a shallow pan and stir over medium-high heat for 3 minutes. Place the whole onion into the same pan and stir until brown.
2. Combine the ox tails and the seasoning ingredients (salt, sugar, MSG (optional), fried ginger roots, fried anise seeds, fried yellow onion and Oriental white radishes) in a pressure cooker. Add 5 cups warm water into the cooker. Cover and cook for 50 minutes over medium heat. Turn off the heat. Cool. Let stand 3 hours.
3. Discard the cooked ginger root, anise seeds and onion from the pressure cooker. Remove any excess fat that rises to the surface. The beef stock should be clear.

4. Add 5 more cups of water to the ox tail pressure cooker and bring to a boil again over high heat. Reduce the heat to medium. Check the seasoning. Uncover and continue to cook for 5 more minutes. Reduce the heat to low to keep the broth warm during the meal.
5. Cook the rice noodles (instructions on packet). Rinse with cold water and drain. Separate the cooked noodles and transfer them to a serving bowl.
6. Combine the herb mixture (diced green onions, diced cilantro and white onion slices) to garnish.
7. In a soup bowl, place some fresh bean sprouts, the cooked rice noodles and the cooked ox tails. Pour the beef broth into the serving bowl. Top with the fresh herb mixture, hot chili paste, Hoisin sauce, and black pepper to taste. Serve warm.

# Boiled Egg Noodles & Seafood

## INGREDIENTS (2 – 3 Servings)

- *Mixed Vegetables*: 1 stalk of celery (sliced), 1 fresh carrot (sliced), ½ can (7 oz) young corns, ½ can (7 oz) abalone mushrooms and ½ can (7 oz) water chestnuts
- ½ yellow onion (sliced), 2 teaspoons salt and 3 teaspoons sugar

  3 rolls (12 oz) fresh egg noodles, 2 tablespoons cooking oil and cilantro to garnish

  10 large fresh shrimp (8 oz) (rinsed, drained and de-veined)

  8 oz fresh scallops (rinsed and drained)

  1 teaspoon olive oil

## DIRECTIONS

1. Using a medium-sized pot, fill warm water to half-full. Bring the water to a boil over medium-high heat and immediately, place the noodles in boiling water and cook for 1 minute. Remove from pot, rinse with cold water and drain. Set aside. Stir-fry with 1 tablespoon cooking oil (optional)

2. Place the mixed vegetables (celery, carrot, corns, mushrooms, water chestnuts) into a microwavable bowl and add 1 teaspoon olive oil to the bowl. Cover and cook in the microwave for 5 minutes. Remove from the microwave. Add ½ teaspoon salt and ½ teaspoon sugar and mix well. Set aside.

3. Pat the shrimp and scallops dry, then season with ½ teaspoon salt and ½ teaspoon sugar. Let stand 5 minutes.

4. Heat 1 tablespoon cooking oil in a large pan over high heat for 3 minutes. Place the scallops into the pan, stirring over high heat for 2 minutes or until golden brown on one side. Turn and cook over high heat for 2 more minutes. Remove the scallops from the pan.

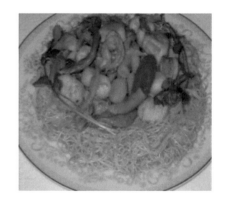

5. Using the same pan, heat 1 tablespoon cooking oil over high heat for 3 minutes. Add the shrimp to the pan, stirring for 1 minute or until golden brown. Turn and cook for another 1 minute. Pour the scallops back into the pan. Add 1 teaspoon salt, 2 teaspoons sugar and onions to the pan. Stir well for 1 minute or until the seasoning is blended. Reduce the heat to medium. Add the cooked mixed vegetables into the pan and stir well for 1 minute. Turn off the heat.

6. Transfer the rice noodles to a serving plate. Top with the cooked mixed vegetables, scallops and shrimp. Garnish with fresh cilantro.

7. Serve warm. Eat with soy sauce and hot chili pepper.

# Boiled Chicken with Rice in Chicken Broth

**INGREDIENTS (3- 4 Servings)**

- 1 (2 lbs) whole chicken (rinsed, drained and cut in ½ ), 2 cups long-grain rice (rinsed, drained)
- 1 stalk green onion, a few strings of cilantro to garnish
- 1 fresh cucumber (sliced) and ½ sweet white onion (sliced)
- *Boiling Ingredients*: 6 cups water, 5 slices fresh ginger root, 1 yellow onion, 2 teaspoons salt and 2 teaspoons sugar
- *Vinegar Salad Dressing*: ¼ cup apple cider vinegar, ¼ cup water, ½ cup sugar and ½ teaspoon salt (combine and mix well)
- *Ginger Sauce*: 4 slices ginger root (thinly cut), 4 tablespoons soy sauce and hot chili paste (combine, mix well and set aside)

**DIRECTIONS**

In a medium-sized pot, bring the boiling ingredients (water, onion, salt, sugar, ginger root) to a boil over high heat. Place the chicken into the boiling water and bring to a boil again. Reduce the heat to medium. Cover and cook for 15 minutes. Turn the chicken and cook for 10 more minutes or until the chicken is tender. Remove the chicken from the pot. Cool and remove excess fat that rises to the surface. Save 3 cups of chicken stock to cook the rice.

Using a rice cooker, combine the long-grain rice and 3 cups of chicken stock. Cook for 15 minutes until the rice is done. Mix gently and keep the rice warm until ready-to-serve.

Remove the chicken bones and place the bones on bottom of a serving plate (optional). Cut the boiled chicken into bite-size pieces. —Stack‖ them nicely on top of the bones (see photo). Garnish with cilantro and green onions.

Arrange the fresh cucumbers and sweet white onions on a serving plate and pour the salad dressing over the salad. Toss gently.

Serve. Dip in ginger sauce and chili hot sauce (optional)

# Barbecue Pork Ribs & Broken Rice

## INGREDIENTS (5 Servings)

- 4 lbs barbecue pork ribs (recipe on page 41)
- 3 cups uncooked broken rice (rinsed and drained)
- 5 whole eggs, 1 tablespoon cooking oil
- fish sauce mix or soy sauce (optional)
- Salad and salad dressing of your choice
- *Oil Mixture Ingredients*: 1 stalk of green onion (chopped), 2 tablespoons olive oil and ¼ teaspoon salt

## DIRECTIONS

1. Cook rice in a rice cooker (instructions on rice packet). Keep rice warm in the rice cooker until ready-to-serve.
2. Prepare the barbecue pork ribs.
3. Prepare the salad and the salad dressing of your choice (lime or vinegar).
4. Heat 1 tablespoon cooking oil in a large pan over medium heat for about 3 minutes. Place one egg at a time into hot pan. Cook the eggs as shown.
5. Prepare the oil mixture: Place 2 tablespoons olive oil into a small microwavable bowl and cook in the microwave for 3 minutes or until the oil is hot. Remove the oil bowl from the microwave and put the chopped green onions into the hot oil. Add ¼ teaspoon salt and mix well. Set aside.
6. Prepare each individual serving: Transfer the cooked broken rice to a serving plate. Add a few teaspoons of hot oil mixture over the rice. Add the barbecue pork ribs and the salad of your choice. Add the cooked egg. Add additional oil mixture to your liking.
7. Serve warm. Eat with fish sauce mix or soy sauce (option).

# Shredded Pork Ham with Rice Sticks & Coconut Milk

**INGREDIENTS (3 - 4 Servings)**

- 1 packet (16 oz) dried rice sticks/vermicelli (large threads)
- 1 lb fresh bean sprouts (rinsed, drained and cook in the microwave for 1 minute)
- 2 tablespoons cooking oil and 5 cloves fresh garlic (chopped)
- 3 lbs fresh pork ham (cut in 4 portions to facilitate fast cooking)
- *Coconut Milk Mixture*: ¾ cup coconut milk, 1 stalk green onion (diced) and ¼ teaspoon salt
- *Boiling Ingredients*: 6 cups of water, a large yellow onion, 4 slices fresh ginger root, 1 teaspoon salt and 1 teaspoon sugar
- *Prepare Salad Mix*: combine ½ bunch of Romaine lettuce (sliced) and 1 large fresh cucumber (sliced)
- *Prepare the Pickles*: 1 fresh carrot (shredded), 1 Oriental white radish (shredded), ¼ cup of apple cider vinegar, ½ cup of sugar and 1 teaspoon salt (combine, mix and let stand 4 hours)

**DIRECTIONS**

Cook rice sticks (instructions on packet). Rinse with cold water and drain. Set aside.

Prepare the boiled pork ham: Bring the boiling ingredients (water, yellow onion, ginger root, salt and sugar) to a boil over high heat. Add pork ham and bring to a boil again. Reduce the heat to medium. Cover and cook for 15-20 minutes until the pork is tender. Remove from pot. Drain and cool.

Heat 2 tablespoons cooking oil in a pan over medium-high heat for 3 minutes. Add chopped garlic to the pan and stir well until golden brown. Place the cooked pork ham into the pan, stirring over medium-high heat for 3 minutes per side until golden brown. Turn off the heat. Cool and cut the cooked pork ham in very thin strings and place into a large serving bowl.

Prepare the coconut milk mixture: Pour the coconut milk into a microwavable bowl and cook in the microwave for 3 minutes. Remove from the microwave. Add the diced green onions and salt. Mix well.

Prepare the individual serving plate: Placing the cooked rice sticks into a serving plate. Pour the coconut milk mixture over the rice sticks. Add the pork ham thinly strings, cooked bean

sprouts, salad mix and the pickles. Eat with fish sauce mix.

# Stir-Fried Tofu & Vegetables

**INGREDIENTS (4 Servings)**

- 1 lb fresh Tofu (firm tofu, cut into cubes)
- ½ lb fresh broccoli (cut into bite-size piecess), ½ lb baby carrots (cut each in ½)
- ½ lb fresh button mushrooms (rinsed and drained), ½ teaspoon salt
- 1 yellow bell pepper (sliced), 1 yellow onion (diced)
- 1 teaspoons salt, 1 teaspoons sugar
- 4 tablespoons cooking oil

**DIRECTIONS**

1. Bring 4 cups warm water and ½ teaspoon salt to a boil over high heat. Place mushrooms into boiling water and bring to a boil again. Reduce the heat to medium. Cover and cook for 15 minutes. Remove the heat and drain.

2. Heat 4 tablespoons cooking oil in a large pan over medium-high heat for 3 minutes. Place ½ the amount of the diced onions into the pan. Add cut carrots, broccoli and the cooked button mushrooms to the pan. Season with ½ teaspoon salt and ½ teaspoon sugar, stirring well over high heat for 5 to 8 minutes or until vegetables are soft, but not mushy. Turn off the heat and remove the cooked vegetables to a large container.

3. Using the same pan and the oil leftover, place the remaining amount of the diced onions, ½ teaspoon salt and ½ teaspoon sugar into the pan. Stir well over medium-high heat for 5 minutes or until the onions turn a light brown. Place the Tofu cubes into the pan and stir in the onions over medium-high heat for 5 minutes, turning occasionally. Repeat the process if needed.

4. Increase the heat to high. Put the cooked vegetables back into the pan. Add the bell pepper slices and mix well over high heat for 2 minutes. Turn off the heat and transfer the stir-fried tofu and vegetables to a serving plate. Garnish with green onions.

5. Serve. Eat with steamed rice, soy sauce and chili hot paste (optional)

# Shredded Pork Ham

## INGREDIENTS (4 Servings)

- 3 lbs fresh pork ham (rinsed, drained and cut into 3 or 4 portions)
- 2 tablespoons cooking oil
- 4 tablespoons coconut soda
- ½ yellow onion (diced), 2 stalks green onions to garnish
- *Boiling Ingredients*: 6 cups cooking water, 1 teaspoon salt, 1 teaspoon sugar, 5 slices fresh ginger root and 1 yellow onion

## INSTRUCTIONS

In a medium-sized pot, bring the boiling ingredients (water, ginger root, salt, sugar, and onion) to a boil over high heat. Place the fresh pork ham into the boiling water and bring to a boil again. Reduce the heat to medium. Cover and cook in the boiling water for 20 minutes or until the meat is tender. Remove from the pot, drain and cool. Set aside.

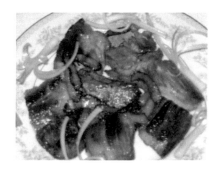

Heat 2 tablespoon cooking oil in a pan over medium-high heat for 3 minutes. Add the diced onions to the pan. Stir until golden brown and transfer the cooked onions to a serving plate. Reduce the heat to medium. Place the cooked pork ham into the pan and stir for 5 minutes per side, turning occasionally.

Add 4 tablespoons coconut soda to the pan. Cover and cook over medium heat until the coconut soda is dried up or until the meat is nicely browned. Turn occasionally. Transfer the cooked pork ham to the cooked onion serving plate (top photo). Garnish with green onions.

Cut the cooked pork ham and serve. Add garlic powder, additional salt and sugar to taste.

Note: you may cut into thinly slices and eat with bread or over rice.

# Shredded Pork Ham with Rice Sticks & Peanuts

INGREDIENTS (4 Servings)

- 1 packet (16 oz) rice sticks/vermicelli (small threads)
- 1 lb fresh bean sprouts (rinsed and drained)
- 2 large cucumbers (diced)
- ½ bunch Romaine lettuce (thinly sliced-optional)
- Shredded pork ham (see recipe page 57)
- Fish sauce mix (see recipe page 38)
- ½ cup ground unsalted roasted peanuts
- *Prepare the Pickles*: 1 fresh carrot (shredded), 1 Oriental white radish (shredded), ¼ cup of apple cider vinegar, ½ cup of sugar, and 1 teaspoon salt (combine, mix and let stand 4 hours)

**DIRECTIONS**

1. Cook the rice sticks (instructions on packet). Rinse with cold water and drain. Place into a large serving bowl or a plate.
2. Prepare the shredded pork ham
3. Prepare the cucumber and radish pickles
4. Prepare the fish sauce mix
5. Combine the diced cucumbers and the fresh bean sprouts. Place into a serving bowl.
6. Prepare an individual plate: To your liking, place a small amount of the fresh bean sprouts into a serving plate. Add carrot and white radish pickles, diced fresh cucumbers, Romaine lettuce slices, and the shredded pork ham. Top with ground unsalted, roasted peanuts.
7. Serve. Eat with fish sauce mix.

# Barbecue Pork with Rice Sticks & Spring Rolls

**INGREDIENTS (4 Servings)**

- Barbecue pork sirloins (recipe page 44)
- Vietnamese Spring Rolls (recipe page 24)
- 1 package (16 oz) rice sticks/vermicelli(small threads)
- ½ cup ground, unsalted roasted peanuts
- Fish sauce mix (recipe page 38)
- *Mixed Vegetables*: 1 lb fresh bean sprouts (rinsed and drained), 2 fresh cucumbers (diced), ½ bunch Romaine lettuce (thinly sliced) and mint leaves (thinly sliced)

**DIRECTIONS**

Prepare the fish sauce mix and set aside.

Prepare the barbecue pork sirloins

Prepare the Vietnamese spring rolls

Cook the rice sticks (instructions on packet). Rinse with cold water, drain and place the cooked rice sticks into a serving bowl.

Combine the mixed vegetables (Romaine lettuce, diced cucumbers, fresh bean sprouts and mint leave slices). Place them into a serving bowl.

Prepare an individual plate: Place the cooked rice sticks into a serving bowl or a plate. Add the barbecue pork sirloins, the spring rolls, and the fresh mixed vegetables. Top with ground, unsalted roasted peanuts.

Serve. Eat with fish sauce mix.

Note: You may add shredded cooked pork ham to this dish.

# Fresh Pork Ham in Coconut Soda

## INGREDIENTS (4 Servings)

- 3 lbs fresh pork ham (use shredded pork ham recipe on page 57)
- 2 tablespoons coconut soda, ¼ teaspoon salt
- 4 loaves of bread (top photo)
- 2 stalks green onions (cut)
- *Mixed Vegetables*: 1 sweet white onion (sliced), ½ small bunch Romaine lettuce (cut into bite-sized portions), 2 carrots (thinly sliced), 2 cucumbers (thinly sliced) and 2 tomatoes (thinly sliced)

## INSTRUCTIONS

1. Prepare the cooked pork ham: use the shredded pork ham recipe on page 57. Add 2 more tablespoons coconut soda and ¼ teaspoon salt.
2. Transfer the cooked pork ham to a serving plate (top photo)
3. Prepare the green onions to garnish
4. Prepare the bread and cut into bite-size pieces.
5. Cut onion into rings
6. Combine the mix vegetables (Romaine lettuce, onions, carrots, cucumbers and tomatoes) and place into a serving plate.
7. Serve with soy sauce.

Note: You may substitute cucumbers for the mixed vegetables or eat with any salad of your choice.

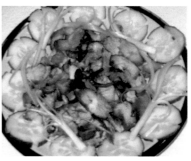

# Mixed Vegetables & Shrimp

**INGREDIENTS (4 Servings)**

- ½ lb broccoli (rinsed, drained, cut into bite-size pieces)
- 10 medium-sized fresh shrimp (rinsed and drained), ¼ teaspoon salt
- ½ whole yellow onion (diced)
- 2 teaspoons salt, 2 teaspoons sugar
- 2 tablespoons cooking oil, 1 teaspoon olive oil
- *Mixed Vegetables*: ½ can (7 oz) young corns, 1 stalk of celery, 1 fresh carrot and 1 tomato (cut into bite-size pieces)
- *Thickening Ingredients*: ½ tablespoon cornstarch and 2 tablespoons water (combine and mix well)

**INSTRUCTION**

1. Remove the shrimp shells and butterfly the shrimp. Leave tails on and devein. Toss the shrimp with ¼ teaspoon salt. Let stand 5 minutes.

2. In a microwavable bowl, combine the mixed vegetables (corn, celery, carrot, and tomato) and cook in the microwave for 3 minutes. Remove from the microwave and add 1 teaspoon salt, 1 teaspoon sugar and 1 teaspoon olive oil to the bowl. Mix well. Set aside.

3. Heat 2 tablespoons cooking oil in the pan over medium-high heat for 3 minutes. Place the diced onions into the pan and stir until golden brown. Add the shrimp to the pan and stir for 1 minute. Add the cooked mixed vegetables to the pan, 1 teaspoon salt and 1 teaspoon sugar and stir well. Mix thickening mixture and slowly pour it into the pan and stir constantly until blended. Check your seasoning. Add additional salt and sugar to your liking.

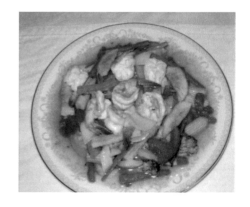

4. Transfer the mixed vegetables and shrimp to a serving bowl. Garnish with cilantro or green onions (optional)

5. Serve. Eat with steamed rice, soy sauce and chili hot pepper.

Note: You may add your choice of cooked meats (cooked chicken rolls were in the photo)

# Stir-Fried Shrimp & Vegetables

## INGREDIENTS (2 servings)

- 16 large fresh shrimp (rinsed and drained)
- ½ sweet white onion (thinly sliced)
- 3 stalks Romaine lettuce (cut each in bite-size pieces)
- 1 fresh cucumber (sliced)
- 2 stalks of green onions (cut to garnish)
- 4 tablespoons cooking oil
- 1 tablespoon tempura batter mix
- Salad of your choice
- *Seasoning Mixture*: ½ teaspoon salt, ½ teaspoon fresh black pepper, ½ teaspoon garlic powder and ½ teaspoon sugar (combine and mix well)

## INSTRUCTIONS

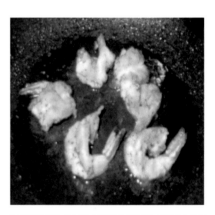

1. Butterfly the shrimp and devein. Keep the shells and the tails on. Sprinkle the seasoning mixture all over the shrimp and mix gently. Sprinkle 1 tablespoon tempura batter mix to both sides of the shrimp. Remove the excess flour before frying.

2. Heat 4 tablespoons cooking oil in a pan over medium-high heat for 3 minutes. Place the coated shrimp into the hot oil, one at a time. Keep the shrimp from curling while cooking. Fry for 1 minute until golden brown. Turn to the other side and fry for another 1 minute. Turn off the heat.

3. Arrange the Romaine lettuce, cucumber and white onion slices on a serving plate. Transfer the fried shrimp from the pan to the serving plate. Top with the remaining sweet onion slices and cut green onions.

4. Serve warm. Eat with steamed rice, salad of your choice, soy sauce and chili hot sauce (optional).

# S        Rice & Chin        Sausage

**INGREDIENTS (2 – 3 Servings)**
- 2 cups uncooked sweet rice (rinsed and drained)
- 2 cups water
- 6 individual Chinese style sausages
- 1 tablespoon all-purpose soy sauce
- 1 stalk of green onion (diced)

**INSTRUCTIONS**

Using a rice cooker, cook the sweet rice with 2 cups water for 15-20 minutes. Mix gently. Leave the sweet rice in the rice cooker until ready-to-serve.

Cut the sausages into bite-size cubes. Place the sausages into a microwavable bowl and cook in the microwave for 2 ½ minutes. Remove excess sausage fat by transferring the cooked sausages over the paper towels, then to the rice cooker.

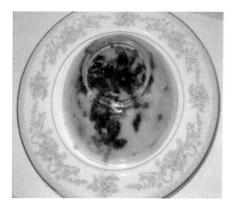

Combine the diced green onions and all-purpose soy sauce. Mix well. Pour the soy sauce and green onion mixture into the sweet rice cooker. Mix well.

Fill a mixing bowl with the cooked sweet rice and sausage mixture (top photo). Press firmly to form a shape and remove the bowl to transfer the rice and sausage mixture to a serving plate (bottom photo).

Serve warm. Add soy sauce to taste.

# and Herbs oy Sa

## INGREDIENTS (2 -3 Servings)

- 1.5 lbs fresh flounder/fluke (cleaned, rinsed and drained)
- 1 teaspoon salt and ¼ teaspoon ground black pepper
- 3 stalks green onions (cut in 3 sections)
- ½ small bunch cilantro (cut in 3 sections)
- 5 slices fresh ginger root (cut into thinly strips)
- 4 tablespoons cooking oil
- *Soy Sauce Mixture*: 2 tablespoons all-purpose soy sauce, 2 tablespoons water, 2 tablespoons sugar, 1 tablespoon olive oil and ¼ teaspoon ground black pepper (combine, mix well and set aside)

## INSTRUCTIONS

1. Cut front and back of the fish to allow the heat to distribute evenly while cooking. Combine 1 teaspoon salt and ¼ teaspoon ground black pepper. Rub both sides of the fish and inside. Let stand 10 minutes.

2. Heat 4 tablespoons cooking oil in a pan over medium-high heat for 3 minutes. Add the ginger root slices to the pan and stir for 1 minute. Place the fish into the pan and cook for 10 minutes or until golden brown. Turn to the other side and cook for another 10 minutes or until fish is fully cooked. Turn off the heat.

3. Remove the cooked fish and the ginger slices to a serving plate. Top with green onions and cilantro.

4. Using the same pan, preheat the pan over medium-high heat for 3 minutes. Pour the soy sauce mixture into the pan and bring to a boil. Turn off the heat. Immediately pour the cooked soy sauce mixture over the fish. Add black pepper to taste (optional)

5. Serve warm. Eat with steamed rice, soy sauce and chili hot sauce.

# Shrimp Fried Rice

## INGREDIENTS (4 Servings)

- 2 cups uncooked Jasmine rice and 3 cups water
- 20 large shrimps (rinsed and drained)
- 4 tablespoons cooking oil
- 1 yellow onion (diced)
- herb salad
- 1 teaspoon salt and 2 teaspoons sugar
- ¼ teaspoon salt and 1 teaspoon garlic powder
- *Egg Mixture*: 2 eggs, ¼ teaspoon salt, ¼ teaspoon olive oil and ¼ teaspoon black pepper

## INSTRUCTIONS

1. Cook the rice with 3 cups water in a rice cooker for 15-20 minutes. Mix gently. Cool.

2. Remove the shrimp shells and devein. Cut each shrimp into bite-size pieces. Toss shrimp with ¼ teaspoon salt and 1 teaspoon garlic powder.

3. Combine the egg mixture (eggs, salt, olive oil and black pepper) and mix well. Set aside.

4. Heat 4 tablespoons cooking oil in a large pan over high heat for 2 minutes. Add the diced onions and stir until the color of the onions changes. Add the shrimp and stir over high heat for 1 minute. Reduce the heat to medium-high. Add the egg mixture to the pan, stirring thoroughly until the egg mixture is separated and cooked. Reduce the heat to medium.

5. Transfer the cooked rice from the rice cooker to the pan and stir over medium heat for 5 minutes or until the color of the rice changes. Add 1 teaspoon salt and 2 teaspoons sugar to the pan and mix thoroughly. Turn off the heat. Remove the fried rice from the pan to a serving plate.

6. Serve. Eat with soy sauce, hot chili paste, and herb salad.

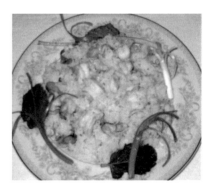

# Roast Duck

## INGREDIENTS (2 Servings)

- ½ whole roast duck (ready-to-eat, available at some Asian food grocery chains, at some Chinese restaurants, or Chinese dim-sum places)
- 3 stalks green onions (cut)
- 6 stems cilantro
- fresh hot peppers
- *Salad*: 1 bunch watercress (rinsed, drained), 1 sweet white onion (sliced ) and 1 fresh cucumber (sliced)
- *Vinegar Salad Dressing*: ¼ cup apple cider vinegar, ¼ cup warm water, ½ cup sugar and 1 teaspoon salt

## INSTRUCTIONS

1. To reheat, place the roast duck skin, the same way as seen in the photo, into a toaster or in the oven for 10 minutes or until heated through. Transfer the roast duck to a serving plate. Discard excess oil. Top with the cut green onions, cilantro, and the fresh hot peppers.

2. Prepare the vinegar salad dressing: combine vinegar, water, sugar and salt in a bowl. Mix well until sugar dissolves.

3. Place the watercress, sweet onions and fresh cucumber slices into a salad serving plate. Pour the vinegar salad dressing over the salad. Garnish with hot chili peppers (optional)

4. Serve. Eat with steamed rice, soy sauce and hot peppers (optional).

# Beef Stew with Carrots

## INGREDIENTS (3 – 4 Servings)

- 1.5 lbs beef for stew
- 1.5 lbs fresh baby carrots (cut each in ½)
- ½ white onion (chopped), ½ white onion(sliced), few stems cilantro
- ½ can (3 oz) tomato paste
- 1 tablespoon cooking oil
- 2 cups water, 2 cups coconut soda
- *Beef Stew Spice Ingredients*: 2 teaspoons salt, 2 teaspoons sugar, 1 teaspoon garlic powder, ½ teaspoon ginger powder, 1 tablespoon olive oil, 1 tablespoon Oriental Beef Spices Powder and 4 cloves fresh garlic (diced)

## INSTRUCTIONS

Combine 1.5 lbs beef stew with the beef stew spice ingredients (salt, sugar, garlic powder, ginger powder, olive oil, beef spices powder, diced garlic). Mix well and let stand 1 hour.

Heat 1 tablespoon cooking oil in a pan over high heat for 2 minutes or until the oil is hot, but not smoky. Place the chopped white onions into the pan and stir until light brown. Add the marinated beef to the pan and stir well over high heat for 10 minutes. Reduce to medium-high heat. Add tomato paste to the pan and stir in with the beef until blended. Turn off the heat.

Combine 2 cups water and 2 cups coconut soda in a medium-sized pot and bring to a boil over high heat. Transfer the cooked beef from the pan to the pot and bring to a boil. Reduce the heat to low-medium. Cover and simmer for 35 minutes then add the carrots to the pot. Continue to cook for 20 minutes or until the meat and carrots are tender. Stir occasionally. Turn off the heat.

Transfer the beef stew from the pot to a serving bowl. Top with the white onion slices and the cilantro. Add some black pepper (optional)

Serve. Eat with bread or steamed rice, salt and black pepper

# Desserts

- Agar in Coconut Milk
- Agar Mix in Fruit Cocktail
- Vietnamese Caramel Custard
- Watermelon and Fruit Cocktails
- Boiled Fresh Chestnuts
- Sweet Mung Beans Soup in Coconut Milk

# Agar in Coconut Milk

## INGREDIENTS (10 Servings)

- ½ oz Agar-Agar (can be found at Asian grocery stores)
- 1 ½ cups sugar, 5 cups water
- 1 can coconut milk (5.5 FL OZ)
- 1 teaspoon banana extract
- 2 large size baking containers (top photo)

## INSTRUCTIONS

Soak the Agar in warm water for at least 30 minutes. Rinse and drain.

Pour 5 cups water into a cooking pot. Place the soaked Agar into the pot. Cover and cook over medium heat for 25 minutes, stirring occasionally until the Agar completely dissolves. Remove any excess Agar that may rise to the surface.

Add sugar to the pot, stirring continuously until sugar dissolves. Add 1 teaspoon banana extract to the pot and mix well. Turn the heat to low.

Prepare a two-layer shape: Transfer ½ the amount of the cooked Agar from the pot to a baking container. Cool for about 30 minutes. Use your finger tip to check the surface occasionally. When the surface of the Agar in the first container is about to thicken, immediately transfer the remaining Agar from the pot to a second baking container. Turn off the heat.

Pour the coconut milk into a small mixing bowl and mix well to eliminate any lumps. Add the coconut milk to the second container and mix it in with the warm Agar until blended, then slowly pour the Agar and coconut milk mixture from the second container over the surface of the first Agar container to form a two-layer shape. Cool. Place in the refrigerator to chill until ready-to-eat.

Serve cold.

Note: You may substitute lemon or vanilla extract for the banana extract.

# Mix in Fruit Cocktails

**INGREDIENTS (10 Servings)**
- 1 Agar Dessert Mix Packet (4.55 oz)
- 2 ¾ cups water
- 2 tablespoons sugar
- 1 can (15 oz) fruit cocktails
- 1 teaspoon sugar

**INSTRUCTIONS**
1. In a cooking pot, empty the content of the Agar dessert mix packet to pot. Add 2 ¾ cups water and 2 tablespoons sugar to the pot and mix well until a smooth surface is formed. Bring to a boil over medium heat, stirring continuously. Bring to a full boil again. Mix well and turn off the heat.
2. Transfer the cooked Agar from pot to a serving bowl. Cool.
3. Place in the refrigerator to chill for 1 hour.
4. Combine 1 teaspoon sugar and fruit cocktails. Discard the juice.
5. Remove the Agar dessert mix bowl from the refrigerator and pour the fruit cocktails over the cooked Agar dessert mix.
6. Serve cold.

Note: You may add your choice of fresh fruits.

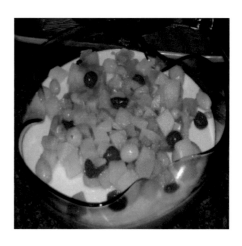

# Vietnamese Caramel Custard

**INGREDIENTS (6 Servings)**

- 3 whole eggs
- 1 tablespoon banana extract
- 3 of 2-serving baking bowls
- ½ cup sugar and 2 cups whole milk
- *Caramel Mixture*: ½ cup of sugar and ¼ cup of warm water

**INSTRUCTIONS**

Prepare the caramel: Combine the caramel mixture (sugar and warm water) in a small cooking pot and mix well until sugar dissolves. Cook over medium-high heat for about 8 to 10 minutes, stirring continuously. Turn off the heat and remove the caramel pot from the stove when the syrup turns deep amber in color. Immediately pour the caramel syrup into each baking bowl and coat the bottom of each bowl evenly. Cool and place the bowls into a large baking container.

Pour 2 ½ cup water into the baking container to prepare for baking. Set aside.

Cook 2 cups of whole milk for 1 ½ minutes. Remove from the microwave and add ½ cup sugar. Mix well until sugar dissolves. Cool and set aside.

In a mixing bowl, whisk the eggs. Add the banana extract to the milk and sugar mixture and combine with the eggs. Mix gently and pour into the caramel coated bowls.

Preheat the oven to 375 degrees. Place the baking container into the oven and bake for 50 minutes or until the custard thickens. Cool and place the caramel custard in the refrigerator to chill.

When it is ready-to-serve, slide a small knife around the side of each custard bowl to loosen and to transfer the caramel custard to a serving plate.

Serve cool.

Note: You may substitute the lemon or vanilla extract for the banana extract.

# Watermelon in Fruit Cocktails

## INGREDIENTS (6 Servings)
- 1 watermelon (3 lbs)
- 1 can (15 oz) fruit cocktails
- 1 teaspoon sugar

## INSTRUCTIONS
1. Cut the watermelon as shown.
2. Remove the flesh of the watermelon, place into a mixing bowl and set aside.
3. In a large mixing bowl, combine the fruit cocktails (discard the juice) and 1 teaspoon sugar. Mix gently.
4. Combine the fruit cocktails and the flesh of the watermelon.
5. Fill the shell of the watermelon with the fruit cocktail and watermelon mixture. Place in the refrigerator to chill until ready-to-eat. Top with mint leaves (optional).
6. Serve.

# Boiled Fresh Chestnuts

**INGREDIENTS (2 Servings)**

- ½ lb fresh water chestnut
- 3 cups water
- ½ teaspoon salt

**INSTRUCTIONS**

1. Bring water and ½ teaspoon salt to a boil over high heat.
2. Add the fresh water chestnuts to the boiling water and bring to a boil again. Reduce the heat to medium and cook for about 25 minutes. Turn off the heat.
3. Transfer the cooked water chestnuts from the pot to a serving plate.
4. Serve.

# Sweet Mung Bean Soup and Coconut Milk

**INGREDIENTS (10 Servings)**

- 1 packet (12 oz) peeled split mung beans (rinsed and drained)
- 1 can (5.5 FL.OZ) coconut milk, ½ teaspoon salt
- ¼ cup tapioca pearls
- 1 cup sugar
- 10 cups water

**INSTRUCTIONS**

1. Soak the mung beans in warm water for 2 hours and drain. In a large-sized pot, bring 10 cups water and the mung beans to a boil over high heat. Reduce the heat to medium. Cover and cook for 30 minutes or until the kernels are open. Stir occasionally.

2. Soak tapioca pearls in warm water for 5 minutes. The water level should cover the tapioca pearls. Discard the water and pour the soaked tapioca pearls into the mung bean pot. Cook for 10 minutes or until the tapioca pearls are clear. Add 1 cup of sugar and cook for 10 minutes over medium heat, stirring occasionally. Reduce the heat to low-medium.

3. In a mixing bowl, combine the coconut milk and ½ teaspoon salt. Mix well to eliminate any lumps and then pour the coconut milk into the pot. Stir well over low-medium heat and bring to a boil again. Turn off the heat.

4. Transfer the sweet mung bean soup to a serving bowl.

5. Serve hot or cold.

# Cooking Steps & Hints

**COOKING STEPS & HINTS**

Cooking Steps/Organization
Green onions
Boiled Wonton Pork Dumplings
Summer Rolls
Ground Beef in Sesame Leaves
Stir-Fried Tofu & Vegetables
Fish & Herbs in Soy Sauce
Fish Preparation
Boiled Fresh Pork Ham
Stir-Fried Linguine & Beef Steaks
Shredded Pork Ham
Bean Threads Soup
Crabmeat & Asparagus Soup
Ground Beef & Rice Soup
Stuffed Tomatoes with Ground Beef
Shrimp with Onions & Hot Peppers
Salt & Pepper Crabs
Squid with Green Onions & Hot Peppers
Stir-Fried Shrimp & Vegetables

Shrimp Fried Rice
Beef Stew with Carrots
Stuffed Pastry Shells with Ground Pork
Agar in Coconut Milk
Vietnamese Caramel Custard

# Cooking Steps/Organization

| | |
|---|---|
| Step 1 | Step 3 |
| Step 2 | Step 4 |

# Green Onions

# Boiled Wonton Pork Dumplings

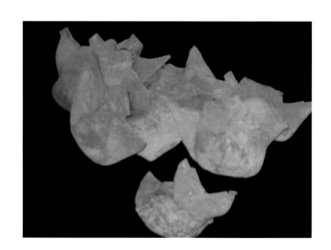

# Summer Rolls

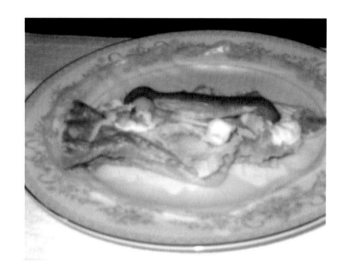

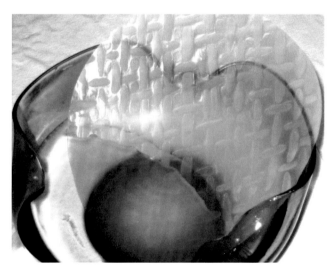

# Ground Beef in Sesame Leaves

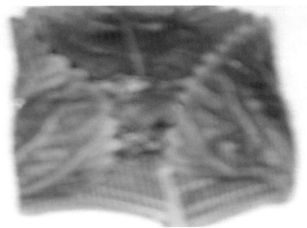

# Stir-Fried Tofu & Vegetables

# Fish & Herbs in Soy Sauce

# Fish Preparation

## INSTRUCTIONS

- The photo shows the fluke. It was cleaned by the grocery store.
- Clean and rinse one more time before cooking
- Drain and cut fish body as shown to ensure the heat is distributed evenly when cooking
- Rub fish with ½ teaspoon salt on both sides and inside of the fish. Brush with 1 teaspoon cooking oil, if desired
- Let stand 15 minutes before cooking.

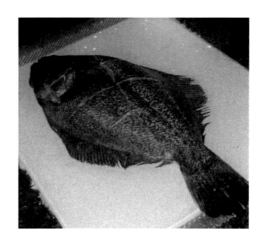

# Boiled Fresh Pork Ham

# Shredded Pork
# Ham

# Stir-Fried Linguine & Beef Steaks

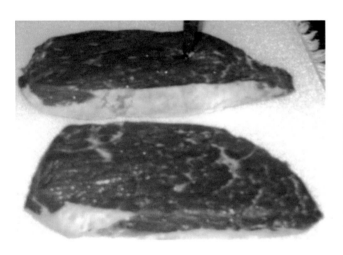

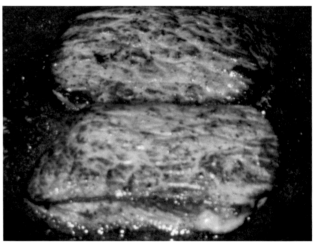

# Bean Threads Soup

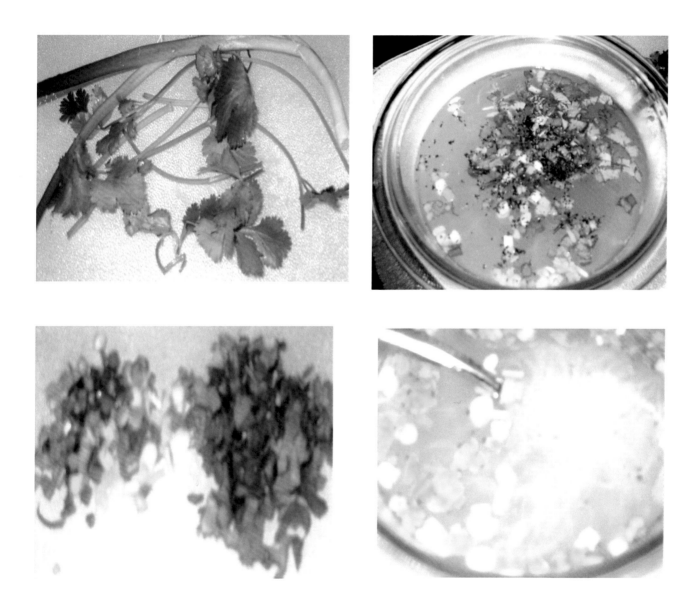

# Crabmeat & Asparagus Soup

# Ground Beef & Rice Soup

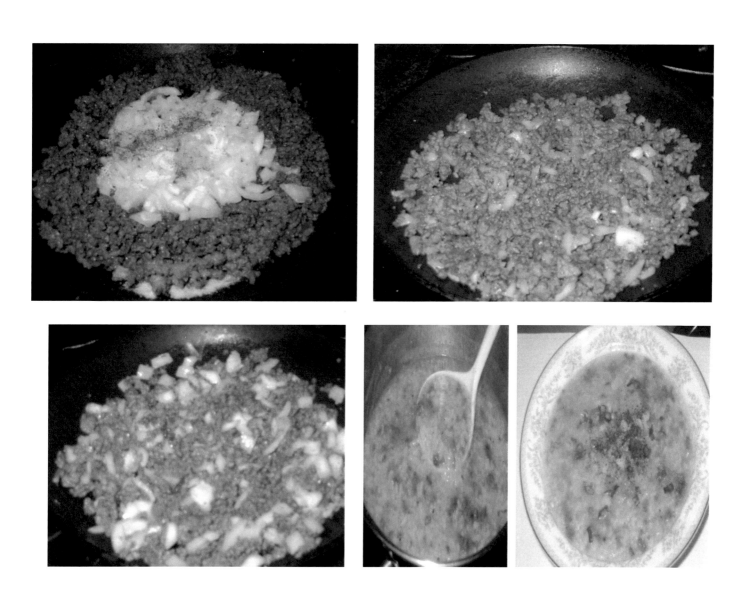

# Stuffed Tomatoes with Ground Beef

# Shrimp with Onions and Hot Peppers

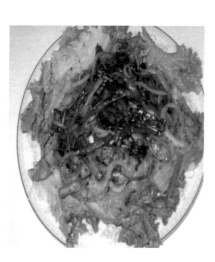

# Salt & Pepper Crabs

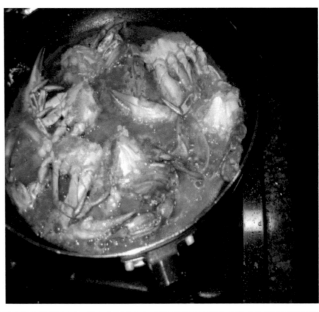

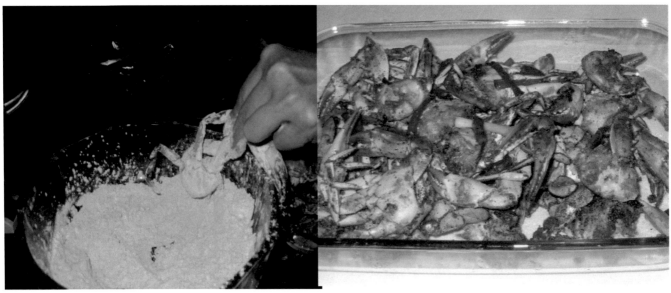

# Squid with Green Onions & Hot Peppers

# Stir-Fried Shrimp & Vegetables

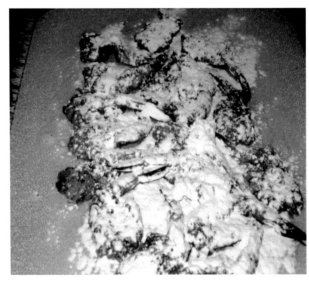

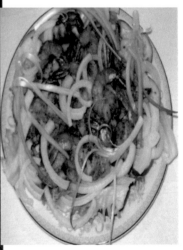

# Shrimp Fried Rice

# Beef Stew with Carrots

# Stuffed Pastry Shells with Ground Pork

# Agar in Coconut Milk

# Vietnamese Caramel Custard

# Products Index

# Products Index

**VEGETARIAN**

# Recipes Index

# Recipes Index

# Technical Index

# About the Author

Dr. Phuong Le Callaway is a native of Vietnam. She was immigrated to the US in 1975, following the Fall of Saigon, South Vietnam. A granddaughter of an original landowner in the South Vietnam and coming from an influential family background in agriculture, politics, military, business and government, she was determined to return to a normal life in the United States. Dr. Callaway was born in the Bac-Lieu province, South Vietnam, and grew up in Saigon at a time when the war situation became dangerous and unbearable for her parents and other family members to remain in the family land region.

Dr. Callaway was Assistant to Associate Managing Director for the National Transportation Safety Board (NTSB) Training Center, located in Ashburn, Virginia before taking a break in Federal service in 2017. She was employed with the U.S. Federal government in 1991 and served in various Federal administrative positions, including Senior Program Analyst and Senior Administrative Officer for the NTSB's Office of Aviation Safety, Resource Manager and Chief, Budget Analyst and Personnel Management Specialist for the U.S. Department of Agriculture. Her assignments included Federal collateral duty positions, covering Equal Employment Opportunity and Civil Rights, Change Agent, Mediator, Workforce Planning, Succession Planning, Strategic Planning, Human Capital Management and Development and served on various committees and taskforces at the Departmental and agency level. Prior to joining the U.S. Federal government, she worked for the Office of Human Resources and the Office of Admissions, Registration and Records at Montgomery College, Rockville Campus, Maryland, for ten years.

She is a Certified Aromatherapist and holds an Associate in Art degree in Accounting, a Bachelor of Science degree in Management and Business, a Master of Science degree in General Administration, Human Resources Management, and a Doctor of Philosophy (graduating with honors) in Organization and Management, with a specialty in Human Resources Management.

Dr. Callaway enjoys cooking and entertaining her family and friends. Her publications to-date include various cookbooks which can be found at www.lulu.com, and www.amazon.com. Her doctoral dissertation, The Relationship between Organizational Trust and Job Satisfaction: An Analysis in the U.S. Federal Work Force was published in 2007 and can be found at, www.universal-publishers.com, and www.amazon.com. Dr. Callaway and her husband currently live in San Antonio, Texas.

# Dr. Phuong Le Callaway's Kitchen

**Dr. Phuong Le Callaway, (Ph.D), CA**

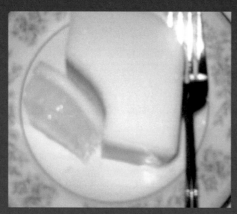

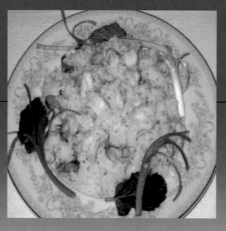